simply chicken

85 delicious everyday recipes

Alberta Chicken PRODUCERS

Recipes by Lovoni Walker Photography by Chris Stambaugh

First published by Alberta Chicken Producers in Canada 2006

Text and recipes copyright 2006 Alberta Chicken Producers
Photographs copyright 2006 Chris Stambaugh
Published 2006 10 9 8 7 6 5 4 3 2 1
Printed in Singapore

Published by Alberta Chicken Producers
#111, 4208 – 97 Street Edmonton, Alberta Canada T6E 5Z9
Tel: (780) 488-2125 Fax: (780) 488-3570
www.chicken.ab.ca

Library and Archives Canada Cataloguing in Publication

Walker, Lovoni, 1965-
    Simply chicken / Lovoni Walker ; Chris Stambaugh, photographer.

Includes index.
ISBN 0-9780176-0-9

    1. Cookery (Chicken). I. Alberta Chicken Producers

TX750.5.C45W34 2006   641.6'65   C2006-900987-2

Recipes & food styling: Lovoni Walker, Fabulous Food Creations Inc.
Photography: Chris Stambaugh, Stambaugh Photographics
Design: Artsmith Communications
Editor: Rendi Dennis
Proof reader: Leanne Taphorn, Fabulous Food Creations Inc.
Kitchen assistant: Amanda Van Unen
Prop stylist: Snez Ferenac, Distinctive Design

We would like to thank the following prop suppliers: Call the Kettle Black, Pier 1 Imports, Stokes, Rafters Home Store, Mikasa Home Store.

We would like to thank Maple Leaf for their generosity in supplying us with the chicken for the testing and photography of this cookbook.

ISBN 0-9780176-0-9

Disclaimer
The recipes and contents in this book have been carefully reviewed and tested. For people with food allergies or people who have special food requirements or health issues, please read each recipe carefully to determine whether or not it may cause a health problem for you. All the information and recipes contained in this cookbook are used at the risk of the consumer. The publisher and author cannot be responsible for any hazards, damage or health issues that may occur as the result of any of the subject matter contained in this cookbook. Please note, the recipes have been tested to ensure their accuracy, however, cooking times are approximate and may vary according to the different ovens, cook tops, pots and pans being used.

Important information: In this cookbook: eggs are large; salt is sea salt; lemon, lime and orange juice are fresh; brown sugar is dark; sour cream is light; parsley is flat leaf; honey is liquid; flour is unbleached.

1 teaspoon = 5ml; 1 tablespoon = 15ml; 1 cup = 250ml

Printed by Star Standard Industries PTE LTD
Trade agent: MRT International Inc. Nisku, Alberta

contents

introduction

It is hard to image a food more versatile than chicken. It is this versatility that allows chicken to be cooked in a multitude of ways, from stir-frying a tender chicken breast to stewing chicken thighs. Apart from its versatility, chicken is also popular for its flavour; ease of preparation and of course its nutritional value, making it a perfect choice for today's health conscience consumer. Chicken is multicultural. Being cooked in almost every country around the world, its mild flavour comes to life when paired with a multitude of spices, herbs and flavourings.

For almost every cooking method you can think of there is a cut of chicken that is perfect to use. A couple of our goals in writing the recipes for 'Simply Chicken' were to use ingredients that you can find in most supermarkets and to showcase chicken in a multitude of ways with some tasty, new recipes proving there is more to chicken than spicy wings, chicken pie and Caesar salad. Still, we have included some favourites. Who doesn't love a whole chicken roasted in the oven until golden brown. Or chicken thighs simmering away in a tasty curry sauce on the cook top. Or marinated and sizzling away on the barbecue.

And who can resist Chicken Noodle Soup to warm your soul? Or Thai–Style, Green Chicken Curry served with a bowl of steaming, hot rice is a delicious and quick meal to prepare. These recipes can be found in the Soups, Stews and Curries section on page 50. We have also included in this section a recipe for making your own chicken broth. Commercial chicken broth works well, especially if only a minimal amount is required. But when you are cooking a soup that requires large amounts of broth, it is important that the broth base be excellent. That is why we recommend taking a little extra time to prepare your own broth. You can freeze it in larger quantities for soups and stews or in ice cube trays to add to sauces and stir-fries.

When you are planning on cooking-up some appetizers you may not have thought of chicken. Chicken makes a great starter because you can pair it with any flavour imaginable. The Chicken Satay recipe on page 21 and Chicken, Herb and Shrimp Cakes on page 19 are sure to become regulars on entertaining menus. Most of the appetizers have handy make-ahead instructions to help with your menu planning.

Many of us are so busy and have limited time to spend in the kitchen. The section called Stir-Fries and One Pot Meals is perfect for rushed people on-the-go. Chicken breasts excel at being fast to cook and delicious to eat so they take centre stage in this section. Try Ginger Chicken on page 75 and Mustard Chicken and Asparagus Toss on page 67. Both are perfect choices for a quick, evening meal.

Chicken is a master at seasonal changes making it perfect to barbecue on a warm summer's day for casual dining. Try the family-favourite, chicken burgers. We have included two delicious ones. Paired with seafood the Chicken and Shrimp Skewers with Peach Salsa are hard to resist.

Chicken goes from the grill to being all dressed up effortlessly in our Entertaining section on page 106. Apricot Glazed Cornish Hens with Hazelnut Stuffing or Roasted Pear and Chicken Salad are sure to impress your guests. With make-ahead instructions and serving suggestions these recipes are sure to help you decide what to cook for your next dinner party.

The Sandwich and Salad section take the humble chicken sandwich to a new level. Make them for weekday lunch or as a light evening meal. Try the Warm Apple and Chicken Salad on page 35 or for something tropical try Chicken Mango Salad on page 36. Chicken salad will never be the same again.

Whatever your taste and no matter how much time you have to spend cooking, bring your kitchen to life with these tried and tested recipes. We are sure the recipes in 'Simply Chicken' will become your favourites. For further culinary inspiration, please visit our website: www.chicken.ab.ca

history

Alberta Chicken Producers is proud to celebrate its 40th Anniversary in 2006. The Board was founded in 1966, led by Howard Falkenberg, who became the first Chair of the Board. Since then, Chairs contributing to the Board's success have been: Albert Tiemstra, Bryan Dillenbeck, Don Sundgaard, Gladwin Toews, David Falkenberg, Ben Luellau, Roger Lavigne, Aaron Falkenberg, and our first-ever female Chair, Sylvia Donkersgoed.

We've had many Directors serving the Board, too numerous to mention, and all of them have in some way contributed significantly to our growth.

General Managers of Alberta Chicken Producers over the past forty years: Wally Landreth, Don Potter, Roger King, Robert Pulyk (Acting) and Lloyd Johnston.

The growth in the Alberta chicken industry has been astounding. Forty years ago, 100 producers marketed 186 thousand birds per week compared to the current 265 chicken producers who market 1 million birds per week. The Alberta chicken industry is value-chain driven where producers work co-operatively with processors, hatcheries, feed industry, suppliers and government. The Canadian structure has proven to be beneficial to all players in the value chain.

Alberta's chicken producers are committed to food safety, bio-security, animal welfare and protecting the environment. Their dedication to the industry and commitment to producing a safe, high quality chicken product ensures consumers a consistent supply of chicken. We look for ways to make our products even better as we respond to evolving consumer preferences.

food safety

When cooking with chicken it is important that proper handling and storage is used to ensure food safety. Salmonella is bacteria that can cause food-borne illness and it is sometimes found on chicken.

HANDLING

A clean work environment is essential to the prevention of contamination when preparing and cooking chicken. Wash hands thoroughly before and after handling chicken. Clean any cutting boards, utensils and work surfaces that have come into contact with the chicken with very hot, soapy water and an antibacterial spray or bleach to prevent the spread of bacteria. When preparing a meal, use a different cutting board for the chicken.

Chicken should be not be exposed to unsafe temperatures for any length of time. In warmer weather, after purchasing chicken from the store, store it in a cooler bag. Take it home and refrigerate or freeze it immediately.

COOKING

Ensure chicken is cooked completely to eliminate any chance of food-borne illness. Check the internal temperate of whole, cooked chicken is 180°F (82°C) when a meat thermometer is inserted into the thigh area. An instant-read thermometer is a good investment. For chicken pieces, the chicken is cooked if the temperature reaches 170°F (77°C) inside and 175°F (80°C) for chicken burgers. Another way to test for doneness is to look for clear juices when the chicken is pierced and meat that is no longer pink inside.

STORING

If you are keeping chicken hot, a temperature of at least 140oF (60oC) must be maintained. When keeping chicken cold a temperature at or below 40oF (4oC) must be maintained.

The amount of time that raw chicken can be refrigerated for depends on how fresh the chicken was when it was purchased. Always check the packing dates. Raw chicken can be kept covered in the refrigerator for up to 3 days. It should be stored away from other foods in the coldest part of the refrigerator. Chicken giblets and ground chicken should be stored for only 1 day. When storing chicken for a longer period of time it should be frozen.

Leftover chicken should be cooled and refrigerated as soon as possible. Chicken should not be left at room temperature for more than 1 or 2 hours. Cooked chicken can be stored up to 3 days in the refrigerator. Leftover cooked chicken can be stored in the freezer up to 3 months.

When freezing chicken, remove it from the packing and rewrap in plastic wrap, waxed butcher's paper or freezer paper twice to prevent freezer burn. Place wrapped chicken in a re-sealable freezer bag. Chicken is best frozen in a flat layer to aid in quick freezing and quick thawing. It is suggested that whole chicken can be frozen up to 1 year and chicken pieces up to 9 months. Giblets and ground chicken up to 3 months. Mark all packages with the date and contents.

THAWING CHICKEN

Chicken can be thawed in the refrigerator on a baking sheet to catch any drips; in cold water in the sink, changing the water about every 30 minutes; or in the microwave on the defrost setting. Remove outer portions as they defrost. Cook microwave-defrosted chicken immediately. It is not advisable to thaw chicken at room temperature. Never freeze previously frozen chicken.

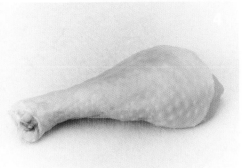

chicken cuts/names

1 whole chicken
2 wing section
3 whole wing
4 drumstick

5 skinless, bone-in breast
6 skinless, boneless breast
7 chicken tender
8 bone-in thigh

9 skinless, boneless thigh
10 skinless, bone-in thigh
11 drumette
12 ground chicken
13 liver

chicken and avocado rice rolls

chicken and avocado rice rolls

Rice paper wrappers and bean thread vermicelli noodles are available in the Asian section of most grocery stores and in Asian markets.

RICE ROLLS
3 oz (90g) bean thread vermicelli noodles
12 rice paper wrappers
1 large ripe avocado, peeled and thinly sliced
1 tablespoon lime juice
1 1/2 cups shredded cooked chicken
1 tablespoon Thai sweet chili sauce
2/3 cup grated carrot
1/4 cup fresh mint leaves

DIPPING SAUCE
3 tablespoons Thai sweet chili sauce
2 tablespoons lime juice
1 tablespoon soy sauce

To make the dipping sauce, combine all the ingredients in a small bowl and set aside.

To make the rice rolls, place the noodles in a medium, heatproof bowl and cover with boiling water. Let stand for 10 minutes; drain. Cut the noodles into 4 inch (10cm) lengths.

Put hot water into a large pie plate. Place one rice paper wrapper into the water. Let stand for about 1 minute or until softened. Carefully remove from the water to a clean, dry work surface, taking care not to tear the delicate wrapper.

Combine the avocado and lime juice in a small bowl. Lay the avocado down the centre of the wrapper, allowing about a 1 1/2 inch (3.5cm) border all around the edge.

Toss the chicken with the chili sauce in a small bowl. Arrange the chicken, noodles, carrot and mint leaves on top of the avocado. Fold in the sides then roll up firmly to enclose the filling. Repeat with the remaining wrappers and filling ingredients. Keep the rolls covered to prevent them from drying out. Serve with the dipping sauce.

Make ahead: The rice rolls can be made 1 hour before serving and stored, covered, in the refrigerator. The sauce can be made a day ahead and stored in an airtight container in the refrigerator.

Makes 12

mini corn cakes with chicken salad

mini corn cakes with chicken salad

Wasabi is available in paste or powder form in the Asian section of most grocery stores and in Asian markets. In this recipe we have used the paste in the tube.

CORN CAKES
2 teaspoons canola oil, plus extra oil for cooking
2 cups corn kernels (fresh, canned or frozen, thawed)
1/2 cup thinly sliced green onion
1/3 cup all-purpose flour
1/2 teaspoon baking powder
1/2 teaspoon baking soda
1/2 teaspoon salt
1/4 teaspoon cracked black pepper
3 eggs, lightly beaten
Lemon slices and fresh cilantro, for serving

CHICKEN SALAD
1 cup chopped cooked chicken
1/3 cup finely chopped cucumber
3 tablespoons egg mayonnaise
1 tablespoon chopped fresh cilantro
2 teaspoons lemon juice
1 teaspoon wasabi paste
salt and cracked black pepper

To make the chicken salad, combine the chicken, cucumber, mayonnaise, cilantro, juice, wasabi, salt and pepper in a medium bowl. Cover and refrigerate until ready to use.

To make the corn cakes, heat 2 teaspoons of the oil in a large frying pan over medium-high heat. Add the corn and green onion and cook, stirring occasionally, for about 3 minutes or until the green onion is softened. Put into a large bowl.

Add the remaining ingredients except for the lemon slices and cilantro, and stir to combine.

Heat the extra oil in a large frying pan over medium heat. Drop tablespoons of the corn mixture into the pan about 2 inches (5cm) apart. Cook for about 3 minutes on each side or until cooked and golden. Remove to a warm plate, cover and set aside. Repeat with remaining corn mixture, adding a little more oil to the pan if necessary.

Place the corn cakes on a serving platter and top with the chicken salad mixture. Garnish with lemon slices and cilantro.

Make ahead: The chicken salad can be made an hour ahead and stored, covered, in the refrigerator. The corn cakes are best made just before serving.

Makes about 18

crispy crumbed parmesan chicken strips

crispy crumbed parmesan chicken strips

Panko breadcrumbs are available in most grocery stores and in Asian markets. Use fine dry breadcrumbs if panko crumbs are unavailable.

1 1/4 cups panko breadcrumbs
3/4 cup finely grated, fresh parmesan cheese
1/2 teaspoon salt
15 chicken tenders (or 3 chicken breasts)*
1/3 cup all-purpose flour
2 eggs, lightly beaten
2 – 3 tablespoons olive oil

CREAMY DIPPING SAUCE
1/2 cup sour cream
1/4 cup freshly grated, fresh parmesan cheese
2 tablespoons lemon juice
3 tablespoons finely chopped green onion
salt and cracked black pepper

Combine the breadcrumbs, parmesan cheese and salt in a medium, shallow dish or on a piece of waxed paper.

Toss the chicken in the flour, then dip into the egg and press into the breadcrumb mixture.

Heat the oil in a large frying pan over medium-high heat. Cook the chicken in 2 or 3 batches, for about 3 minutes each side, adding more oil if needed, or until cooked and golden brown.

To make the creamy dipping sauce, combine all the ingredients in a small bowl. Serve with the chicken strips.

Make ahead: The chicken can be prepared a day ahead and stored, covered, in the refrigerator. The sauce can be made 3 days ahead and stored in an airtight container in the refrigerator.

Serves 4

* If chicken tenders are unavailable use 3 chicken breasts. Remove the tenderloins from underneath each chicken breast and set aside. Cut the chicken breasts lengthways into 4 strips. With the tenderloins, you will have 15 strips.

sun-dried tomato and chicken tartlets

Roasted red peppers are a good alternative to sun-dried tomatoes in this recipe.

13 oz (397g) package ready-made puff pastry, thawed
2/3 cup finely chopped cooked chicken
1/2 cup sun-dried tomatoes in oil, drained and chopped
3 eggs
3/4 cup milk

1/2 teaspoon salt
1/4 teaspoon cracked black pepper
3 tablespoons chopped fresh basil
1/3 cup grated white cheddar cheese

Grease mini-muffin pans (32 holes). Preheat the oven to 375°F (190°C).

Roll out half of the pastry on a lightly floured surface to a 12 inch (30cm) square. Using a 3 inch (8cm) round cookie cutter, cut 16 rounds from the pastry. Press the pastry rounds into the prepared pans. Repeat with the remaining pastry half.

Place the chicken and tomato in each pastry case.

Whisk the eggs, milk, salt, pepper and basil in a 2-cup liquid measure. Carefully pour the mixture into each pastry case. Sprinkle with the cheddar cheese.

Cook, on the bottom rack, in the preheated oven for about 25 minutes or until golden and puffed (the tartlets will deflate on cooling). Let stand in the pan for 5 minutes before removing to a wire rack. Serve warm.

Make ahead: The tartlets can be made up to 1 month ahead and frozen in an airtight container. Heat the tartlets just before serving.

Makes about 32

spicy mustard honey wings

These chicken wings are roasted in the oven producing a delicious alternative to the deep-fried wings so many of us are familiar with.

2 tablespoons dijon mustard
3 tablespoons soy sauce
4 garlic cloves, minced
1 tablespoon finely chopped fresh ginger
2 teaspoons chili powder

1 teaspoon ground cumin
1/2 teaspoon cracked black pepper
2 lbs (1kg) chicken wing pieces and drumettes
3 tablespoons honey
lime wedges, for serving

Combine the mustard, soy sauce, garlic, ginger, chili powder, cumin and pepper in a large, non-reactive bowl or a large, re-sealable plastic bag. Cover or seal and place in the refrigerator for 8 hours or overnight.

Grease a wire rack and place it on a large baking sheet lined with parchment paper. Preheat the oven to 375°F (190°C). Place the chicken in a single layer on the prepared wire rack. Cook in the preheated oven for 35 minutes, turning once during cooking.

Brush the wings with honey and cook for a further 10 minutes or until tender. Serve with lime wedges.

Make ahead: The wings are best marinated a day ahead for maximum flavour.

Serves 4

sun-dried tomato and chicken tartlets

spicy mustard honey wings

chicken and brandy pâté

chicken and brandy pâté

Chicken livers are available fresh or frozen from most grocery stores or specialty food markets.

1 lb (500g) chicken livers
1/4 cup brandy
1/4 cup butter, plus 1/4 cup melted butter
1/2 cup chopped onion
1 garlic clove, minced
1/3 cup whipping cream
1/2 teaspoon salt

1/4 teaspoon cracked black pepper
1 teaspoon chopped fresh thyme
1/4 teaspoon nutmeg
1/2 cup chicken broth (your own,
    see page 61 or store-bought)
1 teaspoon gelatin
thyme sprig

Rinse the livers in cold water and drain. Put the livers in a small bowl and add the brandy. Let stand for 15 minutes. Drain, reserving the brandy.

Heat 1/4 cup of the butter in a medium frying pan over medium-high heat. Add the onion and garlic and cook, stirring occasionally, for about 5 minutes or until the onion is softened.

Add the livers and cook, stirring occasionally, for about 5 minutes or until they are starting to brown. Add the reserved brandy and cook for about 5 minutes or until almost all the liquid is evaporated.

Put the liver mixture, 1/4 cup of melted butter, cream, salt, pepper, thyme and nutmeg into a blender and blend until smooth. Scrape into a 2-cup serving dish or 2, 1 cup dishes. Cover and refrigerate for 1 hour.

Put the chicken broth in a small saucepan and sprinkle with the gelatin. Let stand for 3 minutes or until the gelatin is softened. Stir the mixture over medium-low heat for about 2 minutes or until the gelatin is dissolved.

Place a thyme sprig on the pâté. Carefully pour the broth mixture over the pâté. Cover and refrigerate for at least 4 hours or overnight until set.

Make ahead: The pâté can be made 3 days ahead and stored, covered in the refrigerator.
Serving suggestion: Serve with golden toast triangles or water crackers.

Serves 6 to 8

chicken, herb and shrimp cakes

chicken, herb and shrimp cakes

These shrimp cakes make a perfect appetizer for serving to guests because they are so quick and easy to make.

12 medium shrimp, peeled,
  deveined and halved lengthways
1/2 lb (250g) skinless,
  boneless chicken breasts (or thighs), chopped
1 tablespoon lime juice
1 medium red chili, seeded and chopped
1/4 cup garlic chives (or green onion)
3 tablespoons all-purpose flour
2 egg whites, lightly beaten
salt and cracked black pepper
canola oil for shallow frying

DIPPING SAUCE
1 tablespoon chopped fresh basil
1 tablespoon chopped fresh cilantro
1/4 cup soy sauce
2 teaspoons honey, warmed

Combine the shrimp, chicken, juice, chili, chives, flour, egg white, salt and pepper in a medium bowl.

Heat the oil in a large frying pan over medium heat. Drop tablespoons of the shrimp mixture into the pan about 2 inches (5 cm) apart. Cook for about 3 minutes on each side or until cooked and golden.

To make the dipping sauce, combine all the ingredients in a small bowl. Serve with the shrimp cakes.

Make ahead: This recipe is best made just before serving.

Serves 4 to 6

chicken satay skewers

chicken satay skewers

Don't be concerned by the amount of ingredients. This recipe is easy to make and very tasty. The satay skewers can also double as a main course served with steamed, jasmine rice. Fish sauce is available in the Asian section of most grocery stores and in Asian markets.

12, 8 inch (20cm) wooden skewers
1/4 cup finely chopped shallot
4 garlic cloves, minced
2 teaspoons finely grated ginger
2 teaspoons ground coriander
2 teaspoons ground cumin
1/2 teaspoon ground turmeric
2 teaspoons packed brown sugar
1/2 teaspoon salt
2 tablespoons soy sauce
2 tablespoons canola (or peanut) oil
1 1/2 lbs (750g) skinless, boneless chicken
    thighs (or breasts), cut into strips

PEANUT SAUCE
1 tablespoon canola (or peanut) oil
2 tablespoons finely chopped shallot
2 garlic cloves, minced
1 medium red chili, chopped
1/2 cup crunchy peanut butter
1/2 cup coconut milk (or broth)
1 tablespoon packed brown sugar
1 tablespoon lime juice
1 tablespoon soy sauce
1 teaspoon fish sauce

Soak the skewers in water for at least 30 minutes before using.

Combine the remaining ingredients in a large, non-reactive bowl or re-sealable plastic bag. Cover or seal and place in the refrigerator for 30 minutes.

Preheat the barbecue, electric grill or grill pan to medium-high. Thread the chicken onto the skewers and cook on the preheated, greased grill, turning occasionally, for 7 to 10 minutes or until grill marks appear and the chicken is tender.

To make the peanut sauce, heat the oil in a small saucepan over medium heat. Add the shallot, garlic and chili and cook for 1 to 2 minutes or until fragrant.

Stir in the remaining ingredients. Cook, uncovered, stirring occasionally, for about 3 minutes or until thickened slightly. Serve warm with the satay skewers.

Make ahead: The chicken can be marinated a day ahead and stored in an airtight container in the refrigerator.
Serving suggestion: Serve with sliced cucumber and lime wedges.

Makes 12

chicken and green onion spring rolls

Spring roll wrappers and Chinese dried mushrooms are available in the Asian section of most grocery stores and in Asian markets.

4 Chinese dried mushrooms
1/2 lb (250g) ground chicken
1/3 cup finely chopped green onion
1 teaspoon sesame oil
2 garlic cloves, minced
2 teaspoons finely grated ginger
1/2 cup grated carrot

2 tablespoons chopped fresh cilantro
2 teaspoons finely chopped lemon grass
2 tablespoons soy sauce
2 tablespoons oyster sauce
18, 6 inch (15cm) spring roll wrappers, approximately
1 egg, lightly beaten
oil for deep frying

Put the mushrooms in a medium, heatproof bowl and cover with boiling water. Let stand for about 20 minutes; drain. Remove and discard the stems, finely chop the caps and put into a medium bowl.

Add the chicken, green onion, sesame oil, garlic, ginger, carrot, cilantro, lemon grass and both sauces and mix well.

Lay 4 spring roll wrappers on a clean, dry work surface. Lightly brush the edges of each wrapper with a little egg. Place 2 tablespoons of the filling onto one corner of each wrapper. Fold the same corner over to cover the filling, tuck the sides in and roll-up to enclose the filling. Place on a baking sheet lined with parchment paper and cover with plastic wrap to prevent them from drying out. Repeat with the remaining mixture and wrappers.

Heat the oil in a large wok or pot until hot (350°F/180°C). Deep-fry the spring rolls in batches in the hot oil, for about 2 minutes or until cooked through and golden brown. Drain on paper towel. Serve hot.

Make ahead: The spring rolls can be prepared up to a month ahead, cover and freeze, in a single layer on a baking sheet. Or, they can be prepared a day ahead and stored in the refrigerator.
Serving suggestion: Serve with soy sauce, Thai sweet chili sauce, hot chili sauce or honey mustard for dipping.

Makes about 18

chicken and green onion spring rolls

roasted sweet potato and chicken salad

roasted sweet potato and chicken salad

MUSTARD DRESSING
1/3 cup olive oil
2 tablespoons red wine vinegar
2 teaspoons dijon mustard
1 garlic clove, minced
2 teaspoons packed brown sugar
salt and cracked black pepper

CHICKEN SALAD
1 tablespoon olive oil
3/4 lb (375g) yam (orange sweet potato),
    peeled and cut into 3/4 inch (2cm) cubes
salt and cracked black pepper
2 cups shredded cooked chicken
4 cups mixed baby lettuce leaves (or arugula)
1/2 cup cashews, toasted

To make the mustard dressing, put all the ingredients in a jar and shake until well combined.

To make the chicken salad, line a baking sheet with parchment paper. Preheat the oven to 375°F (190°C).

Combine the oil, yam, salt and pepper on the prepared baking sheet and arrange in a single layer. Roast, uncovered, in the preheated oven, turning once during cooking, for 30 to 40 minutes or until tender and golden.

Put the yam, chicken, lettuce and cashews in a large bowl. Drizzle with the dressing and gently toss.

Make ahead: The dressing can be made a day ahead and stored in a jar in the refrigerator. Remove from the refrigerator 1 hour before serving.

Serves 4

chicken salad sandwiches

chicken salad sandwiches

A perfect sandwich for picnics and weekday lunches.

1 1/2 cups chopped cooked chicken
1/3 cup thinly sliced green onion
1/3 cup finely chopped celery
1/3 cup finely chopped red pepper

1/3 cup whole egg mayonnaise
3 tablespoons whipping cream (or half and half)
salt and cracked black pepper
8 - 12 bread slices of your choice, buttered if desired

Combine the chicken, green onion, celery, red pepper, mayonnaise, cream, salt and pepper in a medium bowl.

Top half of the bread slices with the chicken mixture. Cover with the remaining bread slices.

Make ahead: The filling can be made up to 3 days ahead and stored, covered, in the refrigerator.

Makes 4 to 6

TIP: A store-bought roasted chicken saves time and is quick and easy when a recipe calls for cooked chicken.

chicken lime salad

chicken lime salad

Thai sweet chili sauce and fish sauce are available in the Asian section of most grocery stores and in Asian markets.

CHICKEN SALAD
1 tablespoon canola (or peanut) oil
1 lb (500g) ground chicken
1 teaspoon finely grated ginger
1/2 cup finely chopped red onion
1/2 cup thinly sliced cucumber
1/3 cup peanuts, toasted, coarsely chopped
2 tablespoons chopped fresh mint
2 tablespoons chopped fresh cilantro
lettuce leaves for serving

LIME DRESSING
1/4 cup canola (or peanut) oil
1/4 cup lime juice
2 tablespoons Thai sweet chili sauce
1 tablespoon fish sauce
1 garlic clove, minced

To make the lime dressing, put all the ingredients in a jar and shake until well combined.

To make the chicken salad, heat the oil in a large frying pan over medium-high heat. Add the chicken and ginger and cook, stirring occasionally and crumbling the chicken, for 5 to 8 minutes or until the chicken is cooked and browned. Put the chicken into a large bowl and let cool.

Add the onion, cucumber, peanuts, mint, cilantro and the dressing and gently toss.

Serve on a bed of lettuce leaves or in lettuce cups.

Make ahead: The salad is best made just before serving. The dressing can be made a day ahead and stored in a jar in the refrigerator. Remove from the refrigerator 1 hour before using.

Serves 4

sun-dried tomato and chicken pannini

8 slices crusty bread
2 oz (60g) goat cheese, softened
3 tablespoons basil pesto

1/2 cup sun-dried tomatoes in oil, drained and chopped
1 1/2 cups chopped cooked chicken
softened butter

Spread half of the bread slices with goat cheese. Spread the remaining bread slices with the pesto. Top the goat cheese with tomatoes and chicken. Top with the pesto bread slices.

Spread top and bottom of sandwiches with a little butter.

Place the sandwiches in a preheated pannini press or two-sided sandwich maker. Cook for 3 to 5 minutes or until golden.

Make ahead: The pannini is best made just before serving.
Serving suggestion: Serve with a salad or a cup of hot soup.

Serves 4

chicken and avocado melt

Canned chipotle peppers can be found in the Mexican section in most grocery stores. You only require one pepper in this recipe but the remaining peppers will keep for 2 to 4 weeks in an airtight container in the refrigerator.

1 canned chipotle pepper
1/3 cup whole egg mayonnaise
8 slices of crusty bread such as
ciabatta, toasted

1 ripe avocado, peeled and sliced
2 cups shredded cooked chicken
1/2 cup roasted red peppers, thinly sliced
1 cup grated Swiss cheese

Put the chipotle pepper and mayonnaise in a blender and blend until smooth.

Spread the bread slices with the mayonnaise mixture. Top with the avocado, chicken, roasted peppers and the Swiss cheese. Place on a baking sheet under a preheated broiler and cook for about 2 minutes or until the cheese is melted and golden.

Make ahead: The melt is best made just before serving.

Serves 4

ROASTING PEPPERS TIP: Preheat a broiler, barbecue or grill pan to medium-high heat.

Brush the peppers with oil and place on a baking sheet. Roast under the preheated broiler, turning occasionally, for about 10 minutes or until the skin is blistered and blackened. Place in a large bowl, cover and let stand for 10 minutes.

Peel away and discard the skin from the peppers. Cut open each pepper and scrape out and discard the seeds and membranes. Cut the peppers into thin strips. Place into an airtight container. Add some oil (about 1 to 3 tablespoons) and a pinch of salt and pepper. Store in the fridge until ready to use.

sun-dried tomato and chicken pannini

chicken and avocado melt

cranberry, chicken and brie wrap

cranberry, chicken and brie wrap

6 asparagus spears, trimmed of tough ends
canola oil
2 tablespoons cranberry jelly
2 large flour tortillas

1 cup shredded cooked chicken
2 oz (60g) brie cheese, thinly sliced
salt and cracked black pepper

Preheat a barbecue, electric grill or a grill pan to medium-high. Brush the asparagus with a little oil and cook on the preheated, greased grill for about 5 minutes or until grill marks appear and the asparagus are crisp and bright green.

Spread the jelly over one side of both tortillas. Place the asparagus, chicken and brie down the centre of both tortillas and sprinkle with salt and pepper. Roll up to enclose the filling.

Brush the tortillas with a little oil. Cook on the preheated, greased grill for about 5 minutes on each side or until grill marks appear and the tortillas are crisp. (Or in a two sided grill for about 6 minutes or until crisp).

Make ahead: The wraps are best made just before serving.

Makes 2

TIP: Chicken is an excellent source of lean protein. A 100g serving of skinless, roasted chicken contains 33g of protein.

warm apple and chicken salad

warm apple and chicken salad

We used "blue de bresse," a mild, creamy blue cheese in this recipe.

BLUE CHEESE DRESSING
2 tablespoons finely chopped shallot
1/3 cup canola oil
2 oz (60g) blue cheese, chopped
2 tablespoons white wine vinegar
1 tablespoon honey
salt and cracked black pepper

CHICKEN SALAD
1 tablespoon canola oil
3 medium apples, peeled, cored and sliced
salt and cracked black pepper
2 cups shredded cooked chicken
3 cups baby spinach leaves
1 radicchio lettuce, torn

To make the blue cheese dressing, put all the ingredients in a jar and shake well until combined.

To make the chicken salad, heat the oil in a medium frying pan over medium-high heat. Add the apples, salt and pepper and cook, stirring occasionally, for about 5 minutes or until softened slightly and lightly browned.

Put the chicken, apples, spinach and radicchio in a large bowl. Drizzle with the dressing and gently toss.

Make ahead: The dressing can be made a day ahead and stored in an airtight container in the refrigerator. Remove from the refrigerator 1 hour before serving.
Serving suggestion: Serve with warm rolls and a glass of crisp, white wine.

Serves 6

chicken mango salad

Bean thread vermicelli noodles are available in the Asian sections of most grocery stores and in Asian markets.

CHICKEN MANGO SALAD
canola oil for deep frying
1 oz (30g) bean thread vermicelli noodles, optional
3 cups shredded cooked chicken
2 mangoes, peeled and sliced (or 14oz/398ml can, drained)
2 large oranges, segmented (see tip box, page 107)
3 cups baby spinach leaves
1/3 cup thinly sliced red onion wedges

LIME BASIL DRESSING
3 tablespoons lime juice
1 tablespoon white wine vinegar
1/3 cup canola oil
1/4 cup medium coconut
1 garlic clove
2 tablespoons chopped fresh basil
salt and cracked black pepper
2 teaspoons packed brown sugar

To make the lime basil dressing, put all the ingredients into a blender and blend until smooth.

To make the chicken mango salad, heat the oil in a wok or large, deep frying pan over medium-high heat. Add the noodles to the hot oil (350°F/180°C). Cook for 5 to 10 seconds or until they puff up; drain on paper towel.

Arrange the chicken, mango, orange, spinach and onion on individual serving plates. Drizzle with the dressing and top with the noodles.

Make ahead: The dressing can be made a day ahead and stored in an airtight container in the fridge. The noodles can be made a day ahead and stored, covered, at room temperature. This recipe is best assembled just before serving.

Serves 4 to 6

spicy bean salad

SPICY BEAN SALAD
1 lb (500g) skinless, boneless chicken breasts
canola oil
salt and cracked black pepper
4 cups shredded romaine lettuce
19 oz (540ml) can kidney beans, rinsed and drained
1/2 cup finely chopped red onion
2 medium, ripe tomatoes, chopped
1 cup grated jalapenao jack cheese
1 1/2 cups tortilla chips, crumbled

CILANTRO DRESSING
3 tablespoons sour cream
3 tablespoons lime juice
2 tablespoons chopped fresh cilantro
1/4 cup canola oil
1 garlic clove, minced
1/2 teaspoon ground cumin
salt and cracked black pepper

To make the cilantro dressing, put all the ingredients in a jar and shake until well combined.

To make the spicy bean salad, preheat a barbecue, electric grill or a grill pan to medium-high. Brush each chicken breast with oil and sprinkle with salt and pepper. Cook on the preheated, greased grill for about 5 minutes on each side or until tender. Let stand for 5 minutes before cutting into thin slices.

Place the lettuce on a serving platter. Scatter the beans, chicken, onion, tomatoes and cheese over the lettuce. Drizzle with the dressing and sprinkle with tortilla chips.

Make ahead: The salad is best made just before serving. The dressing can be made a day ahead and stored in a jar in the refrigerator. Remove from the refrigerator 1 hour before using.

Serves 4 to 6

chicken mango salad

spicy bean salad

chicken pita pizzas

chicken pita pizzas

4 pita bread
2 tablespoons olive oil, plus extra for drizzling
1/4 cup sun-dried tomato pesto
1/2 cup finely grated, fresh parmesan cheese,
    plus 1/2 cup extra
2 garlic cloves, minced

1 1/2 cups shredded cooked chicken
1 small yellow pepper, sliced
1 pint (551ml) basket of cherry tomatoes, halved
1/4 cup loosely packed basil leaves, torn
salt and cracked black pepper

Preheat the barbecue to medium-low.

Brush both sides of each pita bread with 2 tablespoons of the oil. Spread one side with the pesto. Sprinkle with 1/2 cup of parmesan cheese, garlic and the remaining ingredients. Sprinkle with the extra parmesan cheese, and drizzle with a little oil.

Place the pitas on the preheated, greased grill. Cook, with the lid down, for about 5 minutes or until the cheese is melted and the bread is crisp.

Make ahead: The pizzas are best made just before serving.
Serving suggestion: Serve with a Ceasar salad.

Makes 4

chicken burgers with roasted red pepper mayonnaise

citrus spiced skewers

chicken burgers with roasted red pepper mayonnaise

CHICKEN BURGERS
4 small skinless, boneless chicken breasts
olive oil
1/4 teaspoon cumin
1/2 teaspoon dried oregano
salt and cracked black pepper
4 whole-grain buns, split
2 medium ripe tomatoes, sliced
2 cups mixed baby lettuce leaves
1/3 cup thinly sliced red onion

ROASTED RED PEPPER MAYONNAISE
1/2 cup chopped roasted red peppers (see page 30)
1/3 cup egg mayonnaise
1/4 - 1/2 teaspoon sambal oelek (chili paste), optional
1/2 teaspoon balsamic vinegar
1 garlic clove, peeled
salt and cracked black pepper

To make the roasted red pepper mayonnaise, put all the ingredients in a blender or food processor and process until smooth.

To make the chicken burgers, preheat the barbeque to medium-high. Place the chicken between layers of plastic wrap. Using the smooth side of a meat mallet or a rolling pin, gently pound the chicken until about 1/2 inch (1cm) thickness. Brush with a little oil and sprinkle with cumin, oregano, salt and pepper. Cook on the preheated grill for about 3 minutes on each side or until tender.

Place the buns, cut side down, on the preheated grill and cook until golden. Spread both cut sides of each bun with the red pepper mayonnaise. Top the bottom half of the bun with the chicken, tomato, lettuce and onion. Add remaining half of bun.

Make ahead: The red pepper mayonnaise can be made a week ahead and stored in an airtight container in the refrigerator.

Serves 4

citrus spiced skewers

1 1/2 lbs (750g) skinless, boneless chicken
    breasts, cut into long strips
1/3 cup Citrus Spice Rub (page 120)

3 tablespoons olive oil
2 tablespoons mango chutney, plus extra to serve
6, 10 inch (25cm) wooden skewers, soaked in water

Combine the chicken, spice rub, oil and chutney in a large, non-reactive bowl or re-sealable plastic bag. Cover or seal. Refrigerate for 8 hours or overnight.

Preheat the barbecue to medium-high.

Thread the chicken onto the skewers. Cook the skewers on the preheated, greased grill, with the lid closed, for 10 to 12 minutes, turning occasionally, or until the chicken is tender. Serve with the extra chutney.

Make ahead: The chicken can be marinated a day ahead and stored in a sealed container in the refrigerator. Serving suggestion: Serve the skewers with cucumber and yogurt and some steamed rice.

Makes 6

TIP: Invest in some metal skewers – they are re-useable, do not have to be soaked in water and won't burn on the barbecue.

deluxe chicken burgers

shrimp and chicken skewers with peach salsa

deluxe chicken burgers

3/4 lb (375g) ground chicken
1/2 cup fine dry breadcrumbs
2 tablespoons Thai sweet chili sauce
2 garlic cloves, minced
1 egg
3 tablespoons chopped fresh parsley or (cilantro)
salt and cracked black pepper

8 pineapple rings
1/3 cup grated white cheddar cheese
3 tablespoons sour cream
3 tablespoons corn relish
4 sesame (or poppy seed) rolls, split,
  toasted and buttered
1 medium ripe avocado, thinly sliced

Preheat the barbecue to medium-high. Combine the ground chicken, breadcrumbs, chili sauce, garlic, egg, parsley, salt and pepper to taste in a large bowl. Shape the mixture into 4 patties. Cook on the preheated, well-greased grill for about 5 minutes on each side until cooked through.

Cook the pineapple on the preheated, greased grill for about 3 minutes each side or until grill marks appear.

Combine the cheese, sour cream and corn relish in a small bowl. Spread both cut sides of each roll with the sour cream mixture. Top the bottom halves of each roll with a patty, 2 pineapple rings, avocado and the top of the rolls.

Make ahead: The burgers are best made just before serving.
Serving suggestion: Serve with corn, tomato and red onion salad drizzled with lime juice and olive oil.

Makes 4

TIP: Have the chicken patties on hand for a quick meal - make double quantity of the patties and freeze the uncooked patties between layers of freezer or parchment paper and store in an airtight container for up to 3 months.

shrimp and chicken skewers with peach salsa

12, 12 inch (30 cm) wooden skewers, soaked in water
2 teaspoons finely grated lime zest
3 tablespoons lime juice
3 tablespoons chopped fresh mint
1 tablespoon canola oil
3 tablespoons jalapeno jelly (spread)
1/2 teaspoon salt
1/2 teaspoon cracked black pepper
3/4 lb (375g) skinless, boneless chicken breasts,
cut into 3/4 inch (2cm) pieces
36 medium raw shrimp, peeled and de-veined
with tails intact

PEACH SALSA
1 1/2 cups chopped peaches
  (fresh, canned or frozen, thawed)
1/3 cup chopped green onion
2 tablespoons lime juice
2 teaspoons canola oil
salt and cracked black pepper

Combine the zest, juice, mint, oil, jelly, salt and pepper in a large, non-reactive bowl or re-sealable plastic bag. Add the chicken and shrimp and stir. Cover or seal and marinate in the refrigerator for 30 minutes.

Preheat the barbecue to medium-high. Thread the shrimp and chicken onto the skewers.

Cook the skewers on the preheated, greased grill for about 10 minutes or until the chicken is tender and the shrimp are cooked.

To make the peach salsa, combine all the ingredients in a small bowl. Serve with the skewers.

Make ahead: The skewers can be prepared a day ahead, covered and stored in the refrigerator. The salsa can be made a day ahead and stored in an airtight container in the refrigerator.
Serving suggestion: Serve with steamed rice and grilled asparagus.

Serves 4 to 6

spice beer chicken

A simple and fun recipe that is perfect for serving on those long, hot summer days.

3 1/4 lbs (1.7 kg) whole chicken
2 teaspoons olive oil
1 teaspoon dry mustard
1 teaspoon garlic powder
1 teaspoon paprika

3/4 teaspoon salt
1/2 teaspoon cracked black pepper
12oz (355ml) can beer
2 rosemary sprigs
2 garlic cloves, minced

Preheat the barbecue to medium-high. Rinse the chicken inside and out with cold water and pat dry with paper towel. Tuck the wings behind. Brush the chicken all over with the oil.

Combine the mustard, garlic powder, paprika, salt and pepper in a small bowl. Rub the spice mixture all over the chicken and inside the cavity.

Open the beer can and pour out half of the beer and reserve for another use. Place the rosemary sprigs and the garlic inside the beer can. Place the chicken cavity over the top of the beer can so about half of the can sits inside the chicken.

Turn one burner off on the barbecue. Place the chicken on the unlit side using the legs and can as a tripod; close the lid. Cook the chicken, using indirect heat, for about 1 1/2 hours or until cooked and the juices run clear the when the chicken is pieced around the thigh bone (or when a meat thermometer reads 180°F (82°C) when inserted into the thickest part of the thigh). Carefully remove the chicken from the barbecue using oven mitts or rubber gloves. Cover with foil to keep warm and let stand for 10 minutes before carving.

Make ahead: This is best made just before serving so the skin is crisp. Although it is also delicious served cold.
Serving suggestion: Serve with grilled asparagus and corn cobs slathered in chili and red pepper butter.

Serves 4

TIP: Whether or not you plan to eat the skin of the chicken, keep it on during grilling, roasting, baking and broiling. The skin aids in keeping the meat from drying out as well as adding flavour.

spice beer chicken

mustard chicken with vegetable parcels

1/4 cup grainy mustard
1 teaspoon finely grated lemon zest
1/2 cup lemon juice
1 tablespoon olive oil
1 tablespoon chopped fresh rosemary
1/2 teaspoon cracked black pepper
2 garlic cloves, minced
4 chicken drumsticks
4 bone-in chicken thighs
2 tablespoons maple syrup

VEGETABLE PARCELS
4 portobello mushrooms
1 red pepper, sliced
1 small leek, trimmed and sliced
12 asparagus spears, trimmed of woody
   ends and cut into 2 inch (5cm) pieces
1 garlic clove, minced
2 teaspoons balsamic vinegar
2 teaspoons olive oil
2 teaspoons maple syrup
salt and cracked black pepper

Combine all the ingredients, except for the syrup, in a large non-reactive bowl or re-sealable plastic bag. Cover or seal. Marinate in the refrigerator for about 8 hours or overnight.

Preheat the barbecue to medium.

To make the vegetable parcels, cut 4 large sheets of heavy-duty foil. Spray the foil with cooking spray or brush with a little oil. Place the mushrooms and remaining ingredients on each foil sheet. Fold up the parcels to secure.

Cook the chicken pieces on the preheated, greased grill, with the lid closed, for about 20 minutes, turning occasionally, until tender. Brush with the maple syrup and cook for a further 5 minutes.

While the chicken is cooking, cook the vegetable parcels over medium heat, with the lid closed, for 10 to 15 minutes or until tender. Serve the vegetable parcels with the chicken.

Make ahead: The chicken and vegetables can be prepared a day ahead and stored, separately, in airtight containers in the refrigerator.
Serving suggestion: Serve with roasted potato or sweet potato topped with yogurt or sour cream and chopped fresh chives.

Serves 4

mustard chicken with vegetable parcels

lemon spiced chicken with apple mint salsa

lemon spiced chicken with apple mint salsa

3 1/4 lbs (1.7 kg) whole chicken
1/2 cup softened butter
1 tablespoon finely grated lemon zest
1 teaspoon ground cumin
1 teaspoon crushed dried chilies
2 garlic cloves, minced
1/2 teaspoon salt
1/2 teaspoon cracked black pepper

APPLE MINT SALSA
1 tablespoon olive oil
3 medium green apples, peeled, cored and chopped
1 teaspoon packed brown sugar
salt and cracked black pepper
1/2 teaspoon ground cumin
2 oz (60g) feta cheese, crumbled
2 tablespoons chopped fresh mint
1 tablespoon lemon juice

Preheat the barbecue to medium-high. Rinse the chicken inside and out with cold water and pat dry with paper towel. Carefully run your fingers underneath the skin of the chicken loosening it from the flesh.

Combine the remaining ingredients in a small bowl. Spread the mixture evenly between the skin and the flesh of the chicken across the breast and legs. Tie the legs together and tuck the wings behind.

Turn one burner off on the barbecue and grease the grill on the unlit side. Cook the chicken, breast side up, on the greased grill, using indirect heat; close the lid. Cook for about 1 1/2 hours or until cooked and the juices run clear when the chicken is pieced around the thickest part of the thigh bone (or when a meat thermometer reads 180°F (82°C) when inserted into the thickest part of the thigh). Cover with foil to keep warm and let stand for 10 minutes before carving.

To make the apple mint salsa, heat the oil in a medium frying pan over medium-high heat. Add the apples and cook for 3 to 5 minutes or until lightly browned. Add the sugar and stir until dissolved.

Place the apples into a medium bowl; let cool slightly. Add the remaining ingredients and stir gently to combine. Serve with the chicken.

Make ahead: The chicken can be prepared a day ahead and stored, covered, in the refrigerator. Remove the chicken from the refrigerator 30 to 60 minutes before cooking. The salsa is best made just before serving.
Serving suggestion: Serve with roasted potatoes and corn.

Serves 4

chicken curry

chicken curry

Curry paste can be found in the Asian section in most grocery stores or in Asian markets. Curry paste is a blend of oils and spices. For this recipe choose from mild, korma or hot curry pastes according to taste.

1 tablespoon canola oil
1 cup chopped onion
2 garlic cloves, minced
2 teaspoons finely grated ginger
3 tablespoons mild curry paste
14 oz (398ml) can coconut milk

1 cup chicken broth (your own, see page 61 or store bought)
1 lb (500g) skinless, boneless chicken thighs, quartered
3/4lb (375g) yam (orange sweet potato), chopped
1/2 cup dark raisins
1/2 cup green peas, rinsed and drained
3 cups baby spinach leaves

Heat the oil in a large frying pan over medium-high heat. Add the onion, garlic and ginger and cook, stirring occasionally, for about 5 minutes or until the onion is softened. Add the curry paste and cook for about 1 minute or until fragrant.

Add the coconut milk and chicken broth and bring to a boil. Reduce the heat to medium and add the chicken, yam and raisins. Cook, uncovered, stirring occasionally, for about 20 minutes or until the chicken is tender.

Stir in the peas and spinach and cook for about 5 minutes or until hot.

Make ahead: The curry can be made 3 days ahead and stored in airtight containers in the refrigerator. Or store in the freezer in airtight containers up to 3 months.
Serving suggestion: Serve the curry with mango chutney, plain yogurt and steamed basmati or jasmine rice.

Serves 6

chicken stew with spicy sausage

hearty chicken pasta soup

chicken stew with spicy sausage

Chorizo sausage is a pork sausage flavoured with garlic, chili powder and other spices. It is available in the deli section of most grocery stores.

1 chorizo sausage, thinly sliced
1 cup chopped onion
6 garlic cloves, minced
1 cup chopped celery
1/4 cup all-purpose flour
1/2 cup dry sherry
1 1/2 cups chicken broth (your own,
   see page 61 or store bought)

4 carrots, peeled and chopped
1 1/2 lbs (750g) skinless,
   bone-in chicken thighs, quartered
3 springs fresh thyme
salt
1/2 teaspoon cracked black pepper
1 cup frozen green peas
1/4 cup sour cream

Cook the sausage in a large pot or Dutch oven over medium heat, stirring occasionally, for about 5 minutes or until browned.

Add the onion, garlic and celery and cook, stirring occasionally, for about 5 minutes or until the onion is softened.

Add the flour and cook, stirring, for 1 minute to cook the flour. Stir in the sherry.

Add the broth, carrots, chicken, thyme, salt and pepper and stir. Cover and bring to a boil then reduce the heat to medium-low. Simmer, covered, for about 20 minutes, stirring occasionally, or until thickened. Remove the stems from the thyme.

Stir in the peas and sour cream. Cook, uncovered, for about 5 minutes or until hot.

Make ahead: The stew can be made 2 days ahead and stored in an airtight container in the refrigerator. Or freeze in an airtight container up to 3 months.
Serving suggestion: Serve with pan-fried polenta, pasta or roasted potatoes.

Serves 6 to 8

hearty chicken pasta soup

1 tablespoon olive oil
1 1/2 cups chopped onion
2 medium carrots, peeled and chopped
1 cup chopped celery
4 garlic cloves, minced
1 teaspoon sambal oelek (chili paste)
2/3 cup dry white wine (or sherry), optional

1 lb (500g) skinless, boneless chicken breasts, chopped
28 oz (796ml) can diced tomatoes, undrained
3 tablespoons tomato paste
1 1/2 quarts (1 1/2 litres) chicken broth
   (your own, see page 61 or store bought)
1 1/2 cups wagon wheel pasta
1/3 cup chopped fresh mint

Heat the oil in a large pot or Dutch oven over medium-high heat. Add the onion, carrots, celery, garlic and sambal oelek and cook, stirring occasionally, for about 10 minutes or until the onion is softened.

Add the remaining ingredients. Cook, uncovered, stirring occasionally, for about 15 minutes or until the pasta is al dente.

Make ahead: The soup can be made 3 days ahead and stored in airtight containers in the refrigerator. Add more chickn broth if needed. Or freeze the soup in airtight containers up to 3 months.
Serving suggestion: Serve the soup with grilled cheese sandwiches.

Serves 6

mediterranean-style chicken stew

mediterranean-style chicken stew

1 tablespoon olive oil, plus 1 tablespoon extra
1 lb (500g) skinless, boneless chicken thighs, halved
2 cups sliced onion
4 garlic cloves, minced
2 teaspoons packed brown sugar
1 tablespoon balsamic vinegar
2 medium red peppers, chopped

2 teaspoons paprika
1 cup red wine
28 oz (796ml) can diced tomatoes, undrained
1 sprig rosemary
2 bay leaves
salt and cracked black pepper

Heat 1 tablespoon of oil in a large pot or Dutch oven over medium heat. Brown the chicken in 2 batches for about 5 minutes each side until browned. Remove the chicken from the pot and set aside.

Heat the extra oil in the same pot over medium-high heat. Add the onion and garlic and cook for 10 to 15 minutes, stirring occasionally, until the onion is golden-brown and softened. Add the sugar and vinegar and stir until the sugar is dissolved.

Add the remaining ingredients. Cover and bring to a boil. Reduce the heat to low and cook for 30 minutes. Cook, uncovered, for a further 20 minutes or until the chicken is tender and the sauce is thickened.

Make ahead: The stew can be made 3 days ahead and stored in airtight containers in the refrigerator. Or store in the freezer in airtight containers up to 3 months.
Serving suggestion: Serve with sautéed broccolini and al dente fettuccine sprinkled with freshly grated parmesan.

Serves 4

TIP: Dark meat, such as thighs and drumsticks, are perfect for casserolling and stewing because the meat stays moist as it cooks.

chicken, mushroom and wild rice stew

1/2 cup wild rice
1 tablespoon canola oil
1 1/2 cups finely chopped onion
1 cup finely chopped celery
3 medium carrots, peeled and finely chopped
4 garlic cloves, minced
4 cups sliced mixed mushrooms
    (such as portobello, cremini, shitake, enoki)
1 cup dry white wine (or sherry)

2 cups chicken broth
    (your own, see page 61 or store bought)
1 lb (500g) skinless, boneless chicken
thighs, cut into 1/2 inch (1cm) pieces
1/2 teaspoon salt
1/2 teaspoon cracked black pepper
1/2 cup jasmine rice
3 tablespoons sour cream

Put the wild rice in a small bowl. Cover with cold water and let stand for 30 minutes. Drain and set aside.

Heat the oil in a large pot or Dutch oven over medium-high heat. Add the onion, celery, carrots and garlic and cook, stirring occasionally, for about 10 minutes or until the onion is softened.

Add the mushrooms and wine and stir until almost all the wine is evaporated. Stir in the broth, chicken, wild rice, salt and pepper. Cover and bring to a boil. Reduce the heat to medium-low and cook, covered, for 20 minutes.

Stir in the jasmine rice. Cover and cook for about 20 minutes or until the rice is tender.

Add the sour cream and stir until well combined.

Make ahead: The soup can be made 3 days ahead and stored in an airtight container in the refrigerator.
Serving suggestion: Serve with steamed broccoli or zucchini.

Serves 4

TIP: When cooking rice or mashed potatoes, use chicken broth instead of water for extra flavour.

chicken, mushroom and wild rice stew

creamy chicken soup

4 bacon slices, chopped
1 tablespoon canola oil
1 1/2 cups chopped onion
1 lb (500g) skinless, boneless chicken thighs, chopped
4 medium potatoes, peeled and chopped
1 quart (1 litre) chicken broth
  (your own, see page 61 or store bought)

1 1/2 cups milk
1/2 teaspoon salt
1/4 teaspoon cracked black pepper
1 cup whipping cream
2 tablespoons sour cream
2 tablespoons chopped fresh dill

Cook the bacon in a large pot or Dutch oven over medium heat for about 5 minutes or until browned. Place the bacon on paper towel and drain the fat from the pot.

Heat the oil in the same pot on medium-high. Add the onion and cook, stirring occasionally, for about 5 minutes or until softened.

Add the chicken and cook, stirring occasionally, for about 5 minutes or until it is starting to brown.

Stir in the potatoes, broth, milk, salt and pepper. Reduce the heat to medium-low. Cook, partially covered, stirring occasionally, for about 25 minutes or until the potato is softened.

Stir in the cream and dill and cook for 2 minutes or until hot.

Make ahead: The soup can be made 3 days ahead and stored in airtight containers in the refrigerator.
Serving suggestion: Serve the soup with buttered sourdough toast and a salad.

Serves 6

green curry chicken

Green curry paste can be found in the Asian section in most grocery stores or in Asian markets.

1 tablespoon canola oil
2 garlic cloves, minced
1 tablespoon julienne fresh ginger
1 1/2 tablespoons green curry paste
14 oz (398ml) can coconut milk
1 cup chicken broth (your own,
  see page 61 or store bought)

1 tablespoon fish sauce
1 teaspoon packed brown sugar
1 lemon grass stalk, trimmed, halved and bruised
1 lb (500g) skinless, boneless chicken thighs, quartered
10 oz (284g) can sliced water chestnuts, drained
1/4 cup fresh basil leaves, torn
1/2 cup frozen green peas

Heat a wok or large frying pan over medium-high heat. Add the oil, garlic, ginger and curry paste and stir-fry about 1 minute or until fragrant.

Add the coconut milk, broth, fish sauce, sugar and lemon grass. Bring to a boil then reduce the heat to medium-low.

Add the chicken and cook, uncovered, stirring occasionally, for about 20 minutes or until chicken is tender and the sauce is thickened slightly. Remove the lemon grass.

Stir in the water chestnuts, basil and peas. Cook for about 3 minutes or until hot.

Make ahead: The curry is best made just before serving.
Serving suggestion: Serve with steamed jasmine or coconut rice.

Serves 4

creamy chicken soup

green curry chicken

chicken noodle soup

chicken noodle soup

Try making your own broth (see this page) for this soup, the end result is worth it. Soup noodles are available in most grocery stores. They are noodles cut into short lengths.

1 tablespoon canola oil
1 1/2 cups chopped onion
1 1/2 cups chopped celery
4 medium carrots, peeled and chopped
2 medium parsnips, peeled and chopped
4 garlic cloves, minced
2 bay leaves

2 quarts (2 litres) chicken broth
  (your own, see below or store bought)
1 lb (500g) skinless, boneless chicken
breasts (or chicken thighs), chopped
1 1/4 cups soup noodles
salt and cracked black pepper

Heat the oil in a large pot or Dutch oven over medium-high heat. Add the onion, celery, carrots, parsnips and garlic and cook, stirring occasionally, for about 10 minutes or until the onion is softened.

Add the bay leaves and broth. Cover and bring to a boil, then reduce the heat to medium-low. Cook for 15 minutes.

Stir in the chicken and cook, covered, stirring occasionally, for 10 to 15 minutes or until the chicken is tender.

Stir in the noodles. Cook for about 5 minutes or until tender. Add salt and pepper to taste. Remove and discard the bay leaves.

Make ahead: The soup can be made 3 days ahead and stored in airtight containers in the refrigerator. Add more broth if needed. Or freeze the soup in airtight containers for up to 3 months.
Serving suggestion: Serve with hot buttered toast.

Serves 6

chicken broth

Making your own chicken broth is easy and inexpensive, and it contains less salt than most commercially prepared broths, although the packages of prepared broth are convenient to have on hand in the pantry.

1 bunch parsley
3 lbs (1.5kg) whole chicken
2 onions, with skin, quartered
4 large carrots, chopped
4 celery stalks, chopped

8 garlic cloves, bruised
3 bay leaves
1 tablespoon black whole peppercorns
salt
4 quarts (4 litres) water

Cut the stems from the parsley and put them into a stock pot or large Dutch oven. Reserve the parsley leaves for another use.

Rinse the chicken inside and out with cold water and add to the pot.

Add the remaining ingredients and bring to a boil over high heat. Then reduce the heat to medium-low. Simmer, uncovered, for 3 hours. Skim-off and discard any residue from the surface as the broth cooks.

Cool the broth slightly before straining it through a fine metal sieve into a large heatproof bowl; discard the solids. Cover the broth with plastic wrap and place in the fridge for 8 hours or overnight.

Carefully scrape and discard any fat from the surface of the broth. Store the broth in 1/2 cup, 1 cup, 2 cup and 1 quart (1 litre) airtight containers. Label each container with the contents, quantity and date; seal and freeze.

Make ahead: The broth can be made 3 days ahead and stored in an airtight container in the fridge. Or store it in the freezer for up to 6 months.
Serving suggestion: Use the broth as a base for soups and add to stews and sauces.

Makes about 3 quarts (3 litres)

chicken with chives and snap peas

chicken with chives and snap peas

Garlic chives or flowering chives have a small bud on the top of each stalk. Their mild flavour is a tasty addition to any stir-fry. They can be found in many grocery stores or in Asian markets. If garlic chives are unavailable use green onions.

1/2 teaspoon salt	1 tablespoon oyster sauce
2 tablespoons dry sherry	1/2 teaspoon sesame oil
1 lb (500g) skinless, boneless chicken breasts, thinly sliced	1 tablespoon canola (or peanut) oil
1 tablespoon cornstarch	1 teaspoon finely chopped ginger
1/2 cup chicken broth (your own, see page 61 or store bought)	2 garlic cloves, minced
	4 oz (125g) sugar snap peas, trimmed
1 tablespoon soy sauce	1/4 cup chopped garlic chives (or green onions)
	1/3 cup whole almonds, toasted

Combine the salt, sherry and chicken in a medium bowl and set aside. Combine the cornstarch, broth, soy sauce, oyster sauce and sesame oil in a small bowl and set aside.

Heat a wok or large frying pan over medium-high heat. Add the canola oil, ginger and garlic and stir-fry for about 1 minute or until fragrant. Add the chicken mixture and stir-fry for 3 minutes.

Add the peas and broth mixture and stir-fry for about 2 minutes or until the chicken is tender and the peas are crisp and bright green.

Add the chives and almonds and stir-fry until combined.

Serving suggestion: Serve with piping-hot, thin rice noodles.

Serves 4

TIP: Stir-fries are best made just before serving.

poached chicken with asian greens

Enoki mushrooms come in clumps of long stems with tiny white caps. They are available in some grocery stores and in Asian markets.

12 Chinese dried mushrooms
4 oz (125g) thin rice stick noodles
1 quart (1 litre) chicken broth
   (your own, see page 61 or store bought)
2 tablespoons oyster sauce
2 tablespoons soy sauce

1 1/2 inch (3.5cm) piece of ginger,
   peeled and thinly sliced
1lb (500g) skinless, boneless chicken breasts, sliced
3 baby Shanghai bok choy, trimmed and separated
3 1/2 oz (100g) enoki mushrooms, trimmed

Place the dried mushrooms in a small, heatproof bowl. Add enough boiling water to cover them and let stand for 20 minutes; drain. Remove and discard the stems and cut the caps in half.

Place the noodles in a large, heatproof bowl. Add enough boiling water to cover them and let stand for 10 to 20 minutes until softened; drain.

Heat the broth, oyster sauce, soy sauce and ginger in a large saucepan over medium heat. Cook, covered, for 5 minutes to infuse the flavours.

Add the chicken and cook, covered, for about 5 minutes or until the chicken is almost tender.

Add the Chinese mushrooms, noodles, bok choy and enoki mushrooms and cook for about 3 minutes or until the chicken is tender and the bok choy is crisp and bright green.

Serving suggestion: This recipe makes a delicious meal served on its own or perhaps try it drizzled with chili sauce.

Serves 4

poached chicken with asian greens

mustard, chicken and asparagus toss

mustard, chicken and asparagus toss

One-pot meals are a synch to make and leave you with virtually no clean-up. This one will be sure to become one of your favourites.

1 tablespoon olive oil
1 lb (500g) skinless,
    boneless chicken breasts, chopped
4 garlic cloves, minced
3/4 lb (375g) baby potatoes, thinly sliced
2 cups chicken broth (your own,
    see page 61 or store bought)

1 tablespoon dijon mustard
1 tablespoon honey
1/2 teaspoon salt
1/4 teaspoon cracked black pepper
1 lb (500g) bunch of asparagus, trimmed of
    woody ends and cut into 1 inch (2.5cm) pieces
3 tablespoons sour cream

Heat the oil in a large frying pan over high heat. Add the chicken and garlic and cook, stirring occasionally, for 5 to 7 minutes or until the chicken is lightly browned.

Add the potatoes, broth, mustard, honey, salt and pepper and cook, covered, for 10 minutes or until the potatoes are tender.

Add the asparagus and sour cream and cook, covered, for 3 to 5 minutes or until the asparagus are crisp and bright green.

Serving suggestion: This recipe is an all-in-one meal but is delicious served with tomato and feta salad drizzled with balsamic vinegar and olive oil.

Serves 4

buttery spinach, chicken and rice

teriyaki pineapple chicken and rice

buttery spinach, chicken and rice

This is a great way to use leftover rice. You can freeze leftover rice in airtight containers for up to 1 month.

2 teaspoons olive oil
1 tablespoon butter, plus 1 tablespoon extra
1 cup chopped onion
2 cups sliced mushrooms
2 garlic cloves, minced
1 lb (500g) skinless, boneless chicken thighs, chopped
2 cups chicken broth (your own,
    see page 61 or store bought)

1 lb (500g) yam (orange sweet potato),
    cut into thin strips
1 1/2 teaspoons chopped fresh thyme
1 teaspoon crushed dried chilies, optional
2 cups cooked jasmine rice
3 cups packed baby spinach leaves
1 1/2 tablespoons lemon juice

Heat the oil and and one tablespoon of butter in a large frying pan over high heat. Add the onion, mushrooms and garlic and cook, stirring occasionally, for about 5 minutes or until the onion is softened.

Add the chicken and cook, stirring occasionally, for about 5 minutes or until chicken is starting to brown.

Stir in the broth, yam, thyme and chilies and cook, uncovered, stirring occasionally, for about 10 minutes or until the yam is softened but not mushy.

Add the rice and spinach and cook, stirring occasionally, for 3 to 5 minutes or until the rice is hot and the spinach is wilted.

Add the lemon juice and extra butter and stir until the butter is melted.

Make ahead: This is best made just before serving although is still delicious as leftovers the next day.

Serves 4

TIP BOX: 1 cup of uncooked jasmine rice yields approximately 3 cups of cooked rice – enough for 4 servings.

teriyaki pineapple chicken and rice

You will need 2 cups of white or brown cooked rice for this recipe.

1 tablespoon canola (or peanut) oil
1 lb (500g) skinless, boneless
    chicken thighs, chopped
1 large red pepper, sliced
1 cup thinly sliced red onion wedges
1 cup pineapple pieces
    (fresh or canned, drained)

1/3 cup teriyaki sauce
1 cup frozen green peas
2 cups cooked jasmine (or brown) rice
1/2 cup sliced almonds, toasted
3 tablespoons shredded fresh basil

Heat a wok or large frying pan over high heat. Add the oil and chicken and stir-fry for about 5 minutes or until the chicken is lightly browned.

Add the red pepper, onion and pineapple and stir-fry for about 3 minutes or until the pepper is crisp and bright.

Add the remaining ingredients and stir-fry for 3 to 5 minutes or until hot.

Serving suggestion: With the rice added to the recipe, this makes a delicious meal on its own.

Serves 4

vindaloo chicken with raisins and cashews

vindaloo chicken with raisins and cashews

Vindaloo curry paste is available in the Asian section of most grocery stores and in Asian markets. Vindaloo is a fiery-hot curry. If preferred, you can use a mild curry paste.

1 tablespoon olive oil
1 cup chopped red onion
2 to 3 tablespoons vindaloo curry paste
1 lb (500g) skinless, boneless
  chicken thighs, chopped
14 oz (398ml) can coconut milk

1/3 cup water
2/3 cup raisins
3 cups baby spinach leaves
19 oz (540ml) can chick peas, rinsed and drained
1/2 cup cashew nuts, toasted

Heat the oil in a large frying pan over medium-high heat. Add the onion and cook, stirring occasionally, for about 5 minutes or until softened.

Add the vindaloo paste and chicken and cook, stirring occasionally, for about 2 minutes or until fragrant.

Add the coconut milk, water and raisins and cook, uncovered, stirring occasionally, for about 15 minutes or until the chicken is tender.

Add the spinach and chick peas and cook, stirring, for about 3 minutes or until the spinach is just wilted.

Stir in the cashew nuts.

Serving suggestion: Serve with steamed basmati rice and crisp pappadums or warm naan bread.

Serves 4

peppery, lemon and chicken stir-fry

For a quick meal, with lots of peppery flavour, cook up this delicious stir-fry in just 15 minutes.

1 tablespoon olive oil, plus 2 teaspoons extra
1 lb (500g) skinless,
    boneless chicken thighs, chopped
4 garlic cloves, minced
1/2 teaspoon cracked black pepper
2 tablespoons chopped fresh mint
1/2 teaspoon sambal oelek (chili paste)

1 teaspoon finely grated lemon zest
1/2 teaspoon salt
1 large red pepper, sliced
1 medium zucchini, sliced
1/3 cup pine nuts, toasted
2 teaspoons lemon juice

Combine 1 tablespoon of the oil, chicken, garlic, pepper, mint, sambal oelek, zest and salt in a medium bowl.

Heat the extra oil in a large frying pan over high heat. Add the chicken mixture and cook, stirring occasionally, for 5 to 8 minutes or until cooked and lightly browned.

Add the peppers and zucchini and stir-fry for 3 to 5 minutes or until crisp and bright.

Stir in the pine nuts and lemon juice.

Serving suggestion: Serve with buttered cous cous, crisp potato wedges or hot penne pasta.

Serves 4

peppery, lemon and chicken stir-fry

ginger chicken

ginger chicken

3 tablespoons soy sauce
3 tablespoons dry sherry
2 teaspoons granulated sugar
1 teaspoon cracked black pepper
1/2 teaspoon salt
1 1/2 lbs (750g) skinless, boneless
  chicken thighs, chopped

1 tablespoon canola (or peanut) oil
1/2 teaspoon crushed dried chilies
1/4 cup finely chopped shallot
1 tablespoon finely chopped ginger
2 garlic cloves, minced
1 teaspoon sesame oil
2 tablespoons rice (or white wine) vinegar

Combine the soy sauce, sherry, sugar, pepper and salt in a bowl or large re-sealable plastic bag. Add the chicken and toss to coat. Cover or seal and marinate in the refrigerator for about 30 minutes or overnight, if time permits.

Heat a wok over medium-high heat. Add the canola oil, chili, shallot, ginger and garlic and stir-fry for about 1 minute or until fragrant.

Increase the heat to high and add the chicken with the marinade. Stir-fry for about 5 minutes or until tender.

Add the sesame oil and vinegar to the chicken and stir-fry for about 3 minutes or until the sauce is thickened.

Serving Suggestion: Serve with steamed Shanghai bok choy or broccoli and steamed rice.

Serves 4 to 6

broccoli, carrot and chicken stir-fry

pear, chili and chicken stir-fry

broccoli, carrot and chicken stir-fry

1/4 cup chicken broth (your own,
   see page 61 or store bought) or water
2 tablespoons soy sauce
2 tablespoons hoisin sauce
2 teaspoons cornstarch
1/2 teaspoon sesame oil
1 tablespoon canola (or peanut) oil
1 lb (500g) skinless, boneless
   chicken breasts, thinly sliced

1 medium onion, cut into thin wedges
2 garlic cloves, minced
1 teaspoon finely chopped ginger
3 medium carrots, peeled and cut
   into julienne strips
3 cups broccoli florets
2 cups sliced mushrooms

Combine the broth, soy sauce, hoisin sauce, cornstarch and sesame oil in a small bowl and set aside.

Heat a wok or large frying pan over high heat. Add the canola oil, chicken, onion, garlic and ginger and stir-fry for 5 to 7 minutes or until the chicken is almost tender.

Add the vegetables and soy sauce mixture and stir-fry until the vegetables are crisp and bright and the chicken is tender.

Serving suggestion: Serve with steamed egg noodles or jasmine rice.

Serves 4

TIP BOX: When making a stir-fry have all the ingredients prepared before you start to cook.

pear, chili and chicken stir-fry

This spicy stir-fry is so simple and quick to make. With few ingredients and quick cooking method it is a perfect meal for busy weeknights.

1/4 cup water
2 tablespoons soy sauce
2 teaspoons cornstarch
1 teaspoon sambal oelek (chili paste)
1/2 teaspoon cracked black pepper
1 tablespoon canola (or peanut) oil

1 lb (500g) skinless, boneless
   chicken breasts, thinly sliced
2 garlic cloves, minced
2 medium firm, ripe pears, peeled, cored and sliced
1 bunch green onions, cut into 1 inch (2.5cm) pieces

Combine the water, soy sauce, cornstarch, sambal oelek and pepper in a small bowl and set aside.

Heat a wok or large frying pan over high heat. Add the oil, chicken and garlic and stir-fry for 5 to 7 minutes or until the chicken is tender.

Add the soy sauce mixture, pears and green onions and stir-fry for about 3 minutes or until the pears are hot and softened.

Serving suggestion: Serve with steamed brown or jasmine rice.

Serves 4

chicken, bean and mushroom stir-fry

chicken, bean and mushroom stir-fry

Sliced zucchini can be used in place of green beans, if preferred.

1 tablespoon canola oil
1lb (500g) skinless, boneless
   chicken thighs (or breasts)
1 bunch of green onions, sliced
2 garlic cloves, minced
2 cups sliced mushrooms
1/4 cup chicken broth (your own,
   see page 61 or store bought)

2 tablespoons jalapeno spread
1 teaspoon cornstarch
1/2 lb (250g) green beans (or a mixture
   of green and yellow)
1/2 teaspoon salt
2 tablespoons shredded fresh basil
1 tablespoon lime juice

Heat the oil in a wok or large frying pan over high heat. Add the chicken, green onions, garlic and mushrooms and cook, stirring occasionally, for about 10 minutes or until the chicken is almost cooked.

Combine the broth, jalapeno spread and cornstarch in a small bowl. Add to the chicken and cook, uncovered, stirring occasionally, for 5 minutes.

Add the remaining ingredients and cook, uncovered, for 3 to 5 minutes or until the beans are crisp and bright green.

Serving suggestion: Served with steamed basmati or jasmine rice.

Serves 4

saffron seafood rice

saffron seafood rice

1/2 teaspoon saffron threads
1 cup dry white wine
1 chorizo sausage, sliced
12 chicken drumettes
1 tablespoon olive oil
1 1/2 cups chopped onion
2 garlic cloves, minced
1 medium red pepper, chopped

3 cups medium grain rice
1 quart (1 litre) chicken broth
  (your own, see page 61 or store bought)
3 medium, ripe tomatoes, chopped
3/4 lb (375g) raw medium shrimp,
  peeled and deveined
10 oz (300g) scallops
1 cup frozen peas

Combine the saffron and wine in a small bowl and let stand for 20 minutes.

Cook the chorizo in a large pot or Dutch oven over medium heat for about 5 minutes or until browned. Remove from the pan and set aside.

Brown the chicken in the same pot, in 2 batches, for about 5 minutes each side or until lightly browned. Remove the chicken from the pan. Drain any the fat from the pot.

Heat the oil in the same pot over medium-high heat. Add the onion, garlic and red pepper and cook, stirring occasionally, for about 10 minutes or until the onion is softened.

Add the rice and stir to combine. Add the saffron mixture and chorizo and stir constantly until almost all the liquid is absorbed.

Add 1 cup of the broth and stir until almost all the liquid is absorbed.

Stir in the remaining broth and chicken. Bring to a boil. Reduce the heat to medium-low, cover and cook for 15 minutes.

Add the tomatoes, shrimp, scallops and peas and cook, covered, for about 10 minutes or until the chicken, seafood and rice are tender.

Make ahead: This recipe is best made just before serving.

Serves 8

spicy chicken noodles

spicy chicken noodles

11oz (340g) fine dried egg noodles
1 tablespoon canola (or peanut oil),
    plus 2 teaspoons oil extra
2 eggs, lightly beaten
4 garlic cloves, minced
1 tablespoon finely grated ginger
2 tablespoons mild curry paste

3/4 lb (375g) skinless, boneless chicken breast, thinly sliced
10 oz (284g) can water chestnuts, drained and chopped
1/2 cup sliced green onion
1/2 lb (250g) medium raw shrimp, peeled and deveined
2 tablespoons soy sauce
2 tablespoons oyster sauce
2 tablespoons dry sherry
1 teaspoon sesame oil

Cook the noodles in a large pot or Dutch oven of boiling, salted water for 5 minutes or until tender.

Heat 1 tablespoon of the oil in a wok or large frying pan over medium high heat. Add the eggs and cook for about 3 minutes or until cooked. Remove from the wok and set aside. Wipe the wok clean.

Heat the extra oil in the same wok over medium-high heat. Add the garlic, ginger and curry paste and stir-fry for 1 to 2 minutes or until fragrant.

Add the chicken and stir-fry for about 5 minutes or until tender.

Add the water chestnuts, green onion and shrimp and stir-fry for about 3 minutes or until the shrimp are almost cooked. Do not over cook.

Combine the remaining ingredients in a small bowl. Add to the chicken mixture with the noodles and eggs. Stir-fry for about 3 minutes or until hot.

Make ahead: The noodles are best made just before serving.

Serves 4 to 6

sun-dried tomatoes and chicken pasta

3 cups penne pasta
1 chorizo sausage, chopped
1 lb (500g) skinless, boneless
  chicken breasts, chopped
4 garlic cloves, minced
1 cup sliced green onion

1 jalapeno pepper, chopped
2/3 cup sun-dried tomatoes in oil, drained and chopped
1 cup whipping cream
1/4 cup coarsely chopped fresh basil
salt and cracked black pepper
2/3 cup finely grated, fresh parmesan cheese

Cook the pasta in a large pot or Dutch oven of salted, boiling water for about 15 minutes or until al dente. Drain the pasta and return to the same pot.

While the pasta is cooking, cook the chorizo in a large frying pan over medium-high heat for about 5 minutes or until browned.

Add the chicken and garlic and cook, stirring occasionally, for about 10 minutes or until the chicken is tender.

Add the green onion, jalapeno pepper and tomatoes and cook, stirring occasionally, for about 5 minutes or until the onion is softened.

Stir in the cream, basil, salt and pepper and cook, stirring occasionally, for 5 minutes or until the sauce is thickened slightly.

Add the chicken mixture and parmesan cheese to the pasta and toss to combine.

Make ahead: The pasta is best made just before serving.
Serving suggestion: This pasta dish is best served with something light and fresh such as a mixed salad of arugula, watercress and pea sprouts salad drizzled white wine vinaigrette.

Serves 6

spinach and chicken cannelloni

1 tablespoon olive oil
4 garlic cloves, minced
1 lb (500g) ground chicken
3 cups baby spinach leaves, coarsely chopped
2 cups ricotta cheese
1/2 cup finely grated, fresh parmesan cheese

1/2 teaspoon ground nutmeg
1/2 teaspoon salt
1/2 teaspoon cracked black pepper
7 oz (200g) package oven ready cannelloni
24 oz (700ml) pasta sauce
1 cup grated mozzarella cheese

Grease a large shallow casserole dish. Preheat the oven to 350°F (180°C).

Heat the oil in a large frying pan over medium-high heat. Add the garlic and chicken and cook, stirring occasionally, for about 10 minutes or until the chicken is cooked.

Stir in the spinach and cook for about 2 minutes or until the spinach is wilted.

Remove from the heat and stir in the ricotta and parmesan cheese, nutmeg, salt and pepper. Stir until well combined.

Spoon the mixture into a re-sealable plastic bag or a piping bag without a nozzle. Snip a corner of the plastic bag and pipe the chicken mixture into each cannelloni shell. Pour 1/3 of the sauce into the casserole dish. Place the cannelloni in a single layer on the pasta sauce.

Pour the remaining pasta sauce over the cannelloni and sprinkle with mozzarella cheese. Bake, uncovered, in the preheated oven for 30 to 40 minutes or until the pasta is tender and the cheese is golden-brown.

Make ahead: The cannelloni can be made 3 days ahead and stored, covered in the refrigerator. Or freeze, covered for up to 3 months.

Serves 4 to 6

sun-dried tomatoes and chicken pasta

spinach and chicken cannelloni

three cheese pasta bake

three cheese pasta bake

4 cups rigatoni pasta
2 tablespoons olive oil
1 1/2 cups chopped onion
3 cups sliced mushrooms
4 garlic cloves, minced
1 lb (500g) skinless, boneless
  chicken breasts, chopped

28 oz (796ml) can diced tomatoes, undrained
1/2 cup sun-dried tomato pesto
salt and cracked black pepper
14 oz (398ml) can artichoke hearts, drained and coarsely chopped
1 cup grated mozzarella cheese
1 cup grated white cheddar cheese
1 cup finely grated, fresh parmesan cheese

Grease a large, shallow casserole. Preheat the oven to 375°F (190°C).

Cook the pasta in a large pot or Dutch oven of boiling, salted water for about 15 minutes or until al dente. Drain and return to the pot.

While the pasta is cooking, heat the oil in large frying pan over medium-high heat. Add the onion, mushrooms and garlic and cook, stirring occasionally, for about 5 minutes or until the onion is softened.

Stir in the chicken and cook, stirring occasionally, for about 10 minutes or until tender.

Add the tomatoes with their juice, pesto, salt and pepper to taste. Cook, uncovered, stirring occasionally, for about 15 minutes or until the sauce is thickened.

Add the artichokes and cook for about 5 minutes or until hot. Add the tomato mixture to the pasta and stir until well combined. Spoon into the prepared casserole and smooth the top.

Combine the remaining ingredients in a small bowl. Sprinkle over the pasta. Bake, uncovered, in the preheated oven for 30 to 40 minutes or until the cheese is golden-brown.

Make ahead: The pasta can be prepared a day ahead and stored, covered, in the refrigerator.
Let stand at room temperature for 1 hour before baking. Or cook, cover and freeze for up to 1 month.
Serving suggestion: Serve with a garden salad and crusty garlic bread.

Serves 6

tomato, white bean and chicken linguine

chicken, raisin and spinach biryani

tomato, white bean and chicken linguine

3/4 lb (375g) linguine
1 tablespoon olive oil
1 lb (500g) skinless, boneless
   chicken breasts, thinly sliced
4 garlic cloves, minced
1 teaspoon sambal oelek
   (chili paste), optional

28 oz (796ml) can tomatoes, undrained
19 oz (540ml) can white beans (such as white kidney
   beans or navy beans), rinsed and drained
1/4 cup chopped fresh parsley
2 tablespoons chopped fresh basil
salt and cracked black pepper
2 tablespoons lemon juice
4 oz (125g) feta cheese, crumbled

Cook the linguine in a large pot or Dutch oven of boiling, salted water, stirring occasionally, for 12 to 15 minutes or until al dente. Drain and return to the same pot.

While the linguine is cooking, heat the oil in a large frying pan over medium-high heat. Add the chicken, garlic and sambal oelek and cook, stirring occasionally, for about 8 minutes or until the chicken is browned.

Add the tomatoes and their juice, beans and cook, stirring occasionally, for 5 to 10 minutes or until the sauce is thickened slightly. Stir in the parsley, basil, salt and pepper.

Add the tomato mixture, lemon juice and feta cheese to the linguine and stir until combined. Serve hot.

Make ahead: The linguine is best made just before serving.
Serving suggestion: Serve with a mixed green salad consisting of sliced cucumber, baby spring leaves, green onion and thinly sliced green pepper drizzled with balsamic vinegar and olive oil.

Serves 4 to 6

chicken, raisin and spinach biryani

1 1/2 lbs (750g) skinless, boneless chicken
   thighs, cut into 1 inch (2.5cm) cubes
2 teaspoons crushed dried chilies
1 teaspoon ground coriander
1 teaspoon ground cumin
1/2 cup plain yogurt
1 teaspoon salt
2 cups basmati rice
2 tablespoons canola oil
2 cups chopped onion

4 garlic cloves, minced
1 cinnamon stick
4 cardamom pods, bruised
3 cups chicken broth (your own,
   see page 61 or store bought)
1/2 cup dark raisins
1 cup frozen peas
2 cups baby spinach leaves
1 cup slivered almonds, toasted

Combine the chicken, chilies, coriander, cumin, yogurt and salt and stir until well combined. Set aside for 30 minutes.

Place the rice in a large bowl and cover with water. Let stand for 30 minutes then drain.

Meanwhile, heat the oil in a large pot or Dutch oven over medium-high heat. Add the onion and garlic and cook, stirring occasionally, for about 5 minutes or until softened.

Add the chicken mixture, cinnamon stick and cardamom pods and stir to combine. Reduce the heat to medium-low and cook, covered, stirring occasionally, for 25 minutes. Reduce the heat to low.

Stir in the rice, broth and raisins. Cover and cook for 20 to 25 minutes or until the rice is tender and the broth is absorbed.

Add the peas and spinach and stir until combined. Remove from the heat. Cover and let stand for about 5 minutes or until the peas are hot and the spinach is wilted.

Remove the cinnamon stick and cardamom pods. Stir in the almonds.

Make ahead: The biryani is best made just before serving but is still good for leftovers the next day.
Serving suggestion: Serve the biryani with mango chutney, plain yogurt and crisp pappadums or warm naan bread.

Serves 6

bacon, mushroom and chicken risotto

bacon, mushroom and chicken risotto

This rich, warming risotto recipe takes a little extra time to make but it is well worth the effort, especially for serving on a cold winter's night.

POACHED CHICKEN
1 lb (500g) skinless, boneless chicken thighs
5 cups chicken broth (your own, see page 61 or store bought)
1 cup red wine

RISOTTO
4 bacon slices, chopped
1 tablespoon olive oil

2 cups sliced mushrooms
1 tablespoon butter
1 cup chopped onion
4 garlic cloves, minced
1 1/2 cups arborio rice
2 teaspoons chopped fresh thyme
1/2 teaspoon salt
1/4 teaspoon cracked black pepper
1 cup frozen green peas
1 cup finely grated, fresh parmesan cheese

To make the poached chicken, cook all the ingredients in a large saucepan over medium heat, covered, for about 25 minutes or until the chicken is tender. Drain the chicken and reserve the poaching liquid and keep hot. Chop the chicken and set aside.

To make the risotto, cook the bacon in a large saucepan over medium heat for about 5 minutes or until browned and slightly crisp. Remove the bacon to paper towel to drain and discard the fat.

Heat the oil in the same saucepan over medium-high heat. Add the mushrooms and cook, stirring occasionally, for about 5 minutes or until lightly browned. Remove from the pan and set aside.

Melt the butter in the same saucepan over medium-high heat. Add the onion and garlic and cook, stirring occasionally, for about 5 minutes or until the onion is softened. Add the rice, thyme, bacon, salt and pepper and stir until the rice is coated.

Reduce the heat to medium. Cook the risotto for 15 minutes, adding the hot, reserved broth mixture, 1 cup at a time, stirring constantly, until almost all the liquid is absorbed before adding another cup.

Add the chicken, mushrooms, peas and any remaining broth mixture. Cook, stirring, for about 5 minutes or until the rice is tender.

Stir in the parmesan cheese. Serve immediately.

Make ahead: The risotto is best made just before serving.
Serve suggestion: Serve with hot crusty bread and a mixed baby spring-leaf salad.

Serves 6

moroccan chicken casserole

moroccan chicken casserole

1 1/2 lb (750g) skinless, bone-in chicken thighs
1 tablespoon olive oil
1 1/2 cups chopped onion
4 garlic cloves, minced
1 teaspoon crushed dried chilies
1 teaspoon ground cumin
1 teaspoon ground coriander
1 teaspoon ground ginger

1 1/2 cups dry white wine
1/2 cup dark raisins
1/2 cup dried apricots, halved
3 tablespoons honey
1 cinnamon stick
1/2 teaspoon salt
1/3 cup large pitted green olives, halved
1/3 cup slivered almonds, toasted

Grease a large, shallow casserole dish. Preheat the oven to 350°F (180°C).

Heat the oil in a large frying pan over medium-high heat. Cook the chicken in 2 batches, for about 5 minutes on each side or until browned. Remove from the pan and place in a single layer in the prepared dish.

Cook the onion and garlic in the same pan over medium-high heat for about 5 minutes or until the onion is softened. Add the spices and cook for about 1 minute or until fragrant. Add to the chicken.

Add the wine, raisins, apricots, honey, cinnamon and salt. Cook, covered, in the preheated oven for 1 1/4 hours.

Stir in the olives. Cook, uncovered, for about 15 minutes or until thickened slightly.

Sprinkle with the almonds.

Make ahead: The casserole can be prepared a day ahead and stored, covered, in the refrigerator. Remove from the refrigerator 1 hour prior to cooking. Or, freeze, covered, for up to 3 months.
Serving suggestion: Add chopped fresh mint and a drizzle of olive oil to hot cous cous.

Serves 4 to 6

chicken and wine casserole

1 1/2 cups (6 oz/185g) sliced pearl onion
1 tablespoon olive oil, plus 1 tablespoon extra
12 skinless, bone-in chicken thighs
4 bacon slices, chopped
4 medium carrots, peeled and chopped
2 garlic cloves, minced
2 cups sliced mushrooms
1 cup red wine

1 cup chicken broth (your own,
  see page 61 or store bought)
2 thyme sprigs
1/2 teaspoon salt
1/2 teaspoon cracked black pepper
1 cup panko breadcrumbs
1 cup grated white cheddar cheese

Grease a large, shallow casserole dish. Preheat the oven to 350°F (180°C).

Heat 1 tablespoon of the oil in a large frying pan over medium heat. Brown the chicken in 2 batches, for about 5 minutes each side until lightly browned; remove from the pan and place in the prepared dish.

Cook the bacon in the same pan over medium heat for about 5 minutes or until browned. Drain the bacon on paper towel and discard the fat from the pan.

Heat the extra oil in the same pan over medium-high heat. Add the onion, carrots, garlic and mushrooms and cook, stirring occasionally, for about 5 minutes or until the mushrooms are softened. Add the bacon and the mushroom mixture to the chicken.

Stir in wine, broth, thyme, salt and pepper. Cook, covered, for about 1 hour or until the chicken is tender. Remove the thyme sprigs.

Sprinkle the casserole with the breadcrumbs and cheese. Cook, uncovered, in 350°F (180°C) oven, for 15 to 20 minutes or until the top is golden brown.

Make ahead: This casserole is best made just before serving.
Serving suggestion: Serve with buttered egg noodles and a Caesar salad.

Serves 6

TIP: To remove the skin from chicken pieces, dredge wet fingers in coarse salt - this enables you to get a firm grip on the chicken. Pull the skin off, using extra salt as required. Discard the skin once it has been removed.

chicken and wine casserole

lemon, potato and chicken casserole

lemon, potato and chicken casserole

3 tablespoons all-purpose flour
8 skinless, bone-in chicken thighs
1 tablespoon olive oil, plus 1 tablespoon extra
1 cup sliced red onion
1 medium leek, trimmed and thinly sliced
4 garlic cloves, minced
1 1/2 cups chicken broth (your own,
    see page 61 or store bought)

1 tablespoon finely grated lemon zest
1/3 cup lemon juice
1 lb (500g) little new potatoes, halved
salt and cracked black pepper
3 medium zucchini, sliced
3 tablespoons chopped fresh parsley

Grease a large, shallow casserole dish. Preheat the oven to 350°F (180°C).

Put the flour and chicken in a large re-sealable plastic bag. Seal the bag and shake to combine. Heat 1 tablespoon of the oil in a large frying pan over medium-high heat. Cook the chicken in 2 batches for about 5 minutes each side until browned. Place in the prepared dish.

Heat the extra oil in the same frying pan over medium-high heat. Add the onion, leek and garlic and cook, stirring occasionally, for about 5 minutes or until softened. Add to the chicken.

Add the broth, zest, juice, potatoes, salt and pepper and stir to combine. Cook, covered, in the preheated oven for about 1 1/4 hours or until the potatoes and chicken are tender.

Stir in the zucchini and parsley. Cook, uncovered, for about 15 minutes or until the zucchini are crisp and bright.

Make ahead: This casserole is best made just before serving.
Serving suggestion: Serve with tomato salad.

Serves 4 to 6

tomato, chili and chicken casserole

1 tablespoon olive oil
8 chicken drumsticks
1 1/2 cups chopped red onion
4 garlic cloves, minced
1/2 to 1 teaspoon sambal olek (chili paste)

3/4 lb (375g) basket cherry tomatoes, halved if large
1 medium red pepper, sliced
1 lb (500g) small baby potatoes, halved
1/2 teaspoon salt
1/4 teaspoon cracked black pepper
1 tablespoon chopped fresh oregano

Grease a medium, shallow casserole dish. Preheat the oven to 350°F (180°C).

Heat the oil in a large frying pan over medium heat. Cook the chicken, in 2 batches, for about 5 minutes on each side or until browned. Place in the prepared dish.

Cook the onion, garlic and sambal oelek in the same frying pan over medium-high heat for about 5 minutes or until the onion is softened. Add to the chicken.

Stir in the remaining ingredients. Cook, uncovered, in the preheated oven, stirring once during cooking, for about 1 1/2 hours or until the chicken and the potatoes are tender.

Make ahead: The casserole is best made just before serving.
Serving suggestion: Serve with grilled polenta and zucchini.

Serves 4

tomato, chili and chicken casserole

roasted chicken with apple stuffing and gravy

3 1/4 lb (1.7kg) whole chicken
2 teaspoons butter, melted
salt and cracked black pepper

GRAVY
1/4 cup all-purpose flour
1/3 cup brandy
1 cup apple juice
1 cup chicken broth (your own,
  see page 61 or store-bought)
1/2 teaspoon salt
1/4 teaspoon cracked black pepper

APPLE STUFFING
2 teaspoons butter
1/2 cup finely chopped onion
1 1/2 cups coarse fresh breadcrumbs (see tip below)
1/3 cup hazelnuts (filberts), toasted and coarsely chopped
1 medium green apple, peeled and coarsely grated
2 tablespoons chopped fresh parsley
salt and cracked black pepper

Grease a wire rack and place it inside a roasting pan. Preheat the oven to 350°F (180°C).

Rinse the chicken inside and out with cold water and pat dry with paper towel.

To make the apple stuffing, melt the butter in a small frying pan over medium heat. Add the onion and cook, stirring occasionally, for about 3 minutes or until softened. Put the onion into a medium bowl. Add the remaining ingredients and mix well.

Spoon the stuffing into the chicken. Secure the opening with toothpicks. Tie the legs together. Tuck the wings behind. Place the chicken on the prepared rack. Brush with the melted butter and sprinkle with salt and pepper. Roast, uncovered, in the preheated oven for about 1 1/2 hours or until cooked and the juices run clear when the chicken is pierced around the thigh bone (or when a meat thermometer reads 180°F (82°C) when inserted into the thickest part of the thigh). Cover with foil to keep warm and let stand for 10 minutes before carving. Reserve any pan juices in the roasting pan.

To make the gravy, remove the wire rack from the roasting pan. Heat the pan juices over medium heat. Add the flour and cook, stirring, for 1 minute. Gradually add the brandy and cook, stirring, until thickened. Add the juice, broth and salt and pepper. Simmer, uncovered, for 5 to 10 minutes or until thickened.

To serve, remove the stuffing from the chicken and cover to keep warm. Carve the chicken and serve with the stuffing and gravy.

Make ahead: The stuffing can be made a day ahead and stored, covered, in the refrigerator. Remove from the refrigerator 1 hour before stuffing the chicken. Stuff the chicken just before roasting.
Serving suggestion: The chicken is delicious served with roasted butternut squash, buttermilk mashed potatoes and steamed sugar snap peas.

Serves 4 to 6

TIP: To make your own breadcrumbs, tear day-old bread into chunks and put in the food processor. Using the pulse action, process until coarse crumbs are formed. The breadcrumbs can then be stored in an airtight container and frozen for up to 3 months.

roasted chicken with apple stuffing and gravy

orange garlic roast chicken

mustard soy chicken thighs

orange garlic roast chicken

1 small orange
3 1/4 lb (1.7kg) whole chicken
4 garlic cloves, bruised, plus 2 garlic cloves, minced
1/2 cup butter
1 teaspoon ground cumin

3 tablespoons chopped fresh cilantro
1 tablespoon chopped fresh mint
1/2 teaspoon salt
1/2 teaspoon cracked black pepper

Grease a wire rack and place it in a roasting pan. Preheat the oven to 350°F (180°C).

Grate 1 teaspoon of zest from the orange and put it in a small saucepan. Cut the orange into quarters.

Rinse the chicken inside and out with cold water and pat dry with paper towel. Put the bruised garlic cloves and orange inside the chicken. Tie the legs together and tuck the wings behind. Place the chicken in the prepared pan.

Melt the butter with the zest over medium-low heat. Add the remaining ingredients. Brush some of the butter mixture over the chicken.

Roast, uncovered, in the preheated oven, brushing with the butter mixture during cooking, for about 1 1/2 hours, or until cooked and the juices run clear when the chicken is pierced in around the thigh bone (or when a meat thermometer reads 180°F (82°C), when inserted into the thickest part of the thigh). Cover the chicken with foil to keep warm and let stand for 10 minutes before carving.

Make ahead: The chicken can be prepared a day ahead. Store, covered, in the refrigerator. Let stand at room temperature for 1 hour before roasting.
Serving suggestions: Serve with mashed, orange sweet potato and steamed green beans.

Serves 4 to 6

TIP: To jazz-up a simple roast chicken, try adding ingredients such as: Lemon, rosemary, garlic, onion, lemon grass and whole spices into the cavity of the chicken. The aromas will permeate through the meat producing subtle but delicious flavours.

mustard soy chicken thighs

2 tablespoons soy sauce
1 teaspoon finely grated ginger
2 tablespoons maple syrup

1 tablespoon grainy mustard
12 bone-in chicken thighs

Grease a wire rack and place it on a baking sheet lined with parchment paper. Preheat the oven to 375°F (190°C).

Combine the soy sauce, ginger, syrup and mustard in a small bowl and set aside.

Place the chicken in a single layer on the prepared rack. Cook in the preheated oven for 20 minutes. Brush with the soy sauce mixture and cook a further 20 to 30 minutes, brushing with the soy sauce mixture during cooking, until the chicken is tender.

Serves 6

devilled chicken casserole

apple and chicken casserole

devilled chicken casserole

3 medium potatoes, peeled and thinly sliced
4 medium carrots, peeled and sliced
1 large onion, peeled and thinly sliced
1/4 cup all-purpose flour
2 tablespoons granulated sugar
1/2 teaspoon salt

1/4 teaspoons cracked black pepper
8 skinless, bone-in chicken thighs
1 cup tomato ketchup
2/3 cup water
1/2 cup Worcestershire sauce
1/3 cup malt vinegar

Grease a large shallow casserole dish with a lid. Preheat the oven to 350°F (180°C).

Put the potatoes, carrots and onion in the prepared dish.

Combine the flour, sugar, salt and pepper in a large re-sealable plastic bag. Add the chicken, seal the bag and shake to coat. Place the chicken on top of the vegetables; sprinkle any leftover flour mixture over the chicken.

Whisk the remaining ingredients together in small bowl and pour over the chicken. Cover and cook in the preheated oven for 1 3/4 to 2 1/4 hours or until the chicken and vegetables are tender.

Make ahead: This casserole can be made up to 3 days ahead and stored covered in the refrigerator. Or, freeze for up to 3 months
Serving suggestion: Serve with sugar snap peas sautéed in olive oil and garlic.

Serves 4 to 6

apple and chicken casserole

8 bone-in chicken thighs
2 tablespoons all-purpose flour
1 tablespoon olive oil
1 medium leek, trimmed and thinly sliced
1/3 cup chopped pancetta (or bacon)
2 rosemary sprigs

1 cup chicken broth (your own, see page 61 or store bought)
1/2 cup white wine
1/2 teaspoon salt
1/4 teaspoons cracked black pepper
2 large green apples, peeled, cored and thickly sliced

Grease a medium, shallow casserole dish. Preheat the oven to 350°F (180°C).

Combine the chicken and flour in a large re-sealable plastic bag; shake to coat.

Heat the oil in a large frying pan over medium-high heat. Cook the chicken in 2 batches, for about 5 minutes, on each side or until browned. Place in the prepared dish.

Cook the leek and pancetta in the same frying pan for about 5 minutes, stirring occasionally, or until the leek is softened. Add to the chicken.

Add the rosemary, broth, wine, salt and pepper and stir to combine. Cook, covered, in the preheated oven for 45 minutes.

Stir in the apple and cook, uncovered, for 15 to 20 minutes or until the apple is softened.
Remove the rosemary sprigs.

Make ahead: This casserole is best made just before serving.
Serving suggestion: Serve with roasted butternut squash and green peas.

Serves 4

grapefruit and warm chicken salad

grapefruit and warm chicken salad

Citrus and chicken make a delicious combination. Serving individual salads in glasses makes a stunning presentation.

GRAPEFRUIT AND CHICKEN SALAD
1 lb (500g) skinless, boneless chicken breasts
salt and cracked black pepper
1 tablespoon olive oil
2 medium red grapefruit, segmented (see Tip below)
4 1/2 cups baby spinach leaves
1/3 cup pistachio nuts, toasted and coarsely chopped
1/2 cup parmesan cheese shavings
1/4 cup fresh mint leaves
1/4 cup pomegranate seeds, optional

HONEY VINAIGRETTE
1/4 cup olive oil
2 tablespoons white wine vinegar
1 tablespoon grainy mustard
2 tablespoons honey
salt and cracked black pepper

To make the honey vinaigrette, put all the ingredients in a jar and shake well until combined.

To make the grapefruit and chicken salad, place the chicken between 2 layers of plastic wrap. Using a rolling pin or the smooth side of a meat mallet, pound until about 1/2 inch (1cm) thickness. Sprinkle with salt and pepper. Heat the oil in a large frying pan over medium-high heat. Cook the chicken for about 5 minutes on each side or until browned and tender. Shred the chicken.

Arrange the chicken and the remaining ingredients on individual serving plates or dishes. Drizzle with the vinaigrette just before serving.

Make ahead: The vinaigrette can be made 3 days ahead and stored in an airtight container in the refrigerator. Remove from the refrigerator just before serving.
Serving suggestion: Serve with some crusty bread and a crisp white wine.

Serves 4

TIP: To segment grapefruit, cut both ends from the fruit. Place the fruit cut-side down on a cutting board. Using a utility or paring knife, cut down and around the fruit, following the shape of the fruit and removing as much of the white pith with the skin as possible.

Place a bowl underneath the fruit to catch any juice. Cut between the membranes of each segment and let them drop into the bowl.

chicken ravioli with almond dill butter

This is perfect for serving as an appetizer or a light lunch. Wonton wrappers are available in the freezer or refrigerator of most grocery stores and in Asian markets.

CHICKEN RAVIOLI
1 tablespoon butter
1/2 cup finely chopped leek
1 cup finely chopped butternut squash
1 cup chicken broth (your own, see page 61 or store bought)
1/4 lb (125g) ground chicken
salt and cracked black pepper
36 wonton wrappers (approximately)
1 egg, lightly beaten

ALMOND DILL BUTTER
1/4 cup butter
3 tablespoons sliced almonds
1 tablespoon chopped fresh dill

To make the chicken ravioli, melt the butter in a medium frying pan over medium heat. Add the leek and cook, stirring occasionally, for about 5 minutes or until the leek is golden and softened.

Add the squash and broth and cook, uncovered, for about 10 minutes or until tender and the liquid is evaporated; cool.

Combine the chicken, salt, pepper and squash mixture together in a medium bowl.

Place 1/4 of the wontons on a work surface. Brush the edge of each wrapper with a little egg.
Place a rounded tablespoon of mixture in the centre of each wrapper. Place another wrapper on top and press the edges together to seal. Repeat with the remaining wrappers, chicken mixture and egg.

Cook the ravioli in a large pot or Dutch oven of salted boiling water for 3 to 5 minutes or until tender and cooked; drain well.

To make almond and dill butter, melt the butter in a small saucepan over medium heat. Add the almonds and cook, stirring occasionally, for about 2 minutes or until the mixture is starting to brown. Remove from the heat and stir in the dill.

Make ahead: The ravioli can be made a day ahead and stored, covered in the refrigerator.
Serving suggestion: Serve with a mixed baby lettuce salad drizzled with balsamic vinaigrette.

Serves 4 to 6

chicken ravioli with almond dill butter

cheese and spinach chicken roulade

4 skinless, boneless chicken breasts
1/4 cup sun-dried tomato pesto
3 oz (90g) goat cheese, softened
1/2 cup baby spinach leaves, stalks removed

1/2 cup grated mozzarella cheese
salt and cracked black pepper
1 tablespoon olive oil

Grease a baking sheet. Preheat the oven to 350°F (180°C).

Remove the tenderloins from each chicken breast and reserve for another use. Place the chicken breasts between layers of plastic wrap and pound until about 1/4 inch (6mm) thickness.

Spread the pesto over the underside of each piece of chicken then sprinkle or spread with goat cheese. Layer with the spinach then sprinkle with mozzarella cheese. Roll up to enclose the filling and secure with toothpicks. Sprinkle with salt and pepper.

Heat the oil in a large frying pan over medium heat. Cook the roulades for 5 to 8 minutes or until browned all over. Place on the prepared baking sheet. Cook, uncovered, in the preheated oven for about 20 minutes or until tender. Cut each roulade into 3 pieces to serve.

Make ahead: The roulades can be prepared a day ahead and stored covered in the refrigerator. Remove from the refrigerator about 30 minutes before cooking. Cook just before serving.
Serving suggestion: Serve with creamy polenta and steamed green beans.

Serves 4

mango chicken pastries

Patty (vol-au-vent) shells are available in the freezer section of most grocery stores.

9 1/2 oz (300g) patty shells
1 tablespoon butter
1/3 cup chopped green onion
1 1/2 tablespoons all-purpose flour
1 teaspoon dijon mustard
salt and cracked black pepper

1 1/4 cups half and half (10% MF)
2 cups chopped cooked chicken
1 cup chopped mango (fresh, canned or frozen, thawed)
1/2 cup finely grated fresh parmesan cheese
2 teaspoons lemon juice

Lightly grease a large baking sheet. Preheat the oven to 400°F (200°C).

Place the patty shells on the prepared baking sheet. Bake in the preheated oven according to package directions.

Melt the butter in a medium saucepan over medium heat. Add the green onion and cook for about 3 minutes or until softened.

Add the flour and stir for 1 minute.

Add the mustard, salt, pepper and half and half. Cook, stirring, for about 3 minutes or until thickened.

Add the chicken and mango and cook, stirring occasionally, for about 5 minutes or until hot. Remove from the heat and stir in the parmesan cheese and juice.

Cut around the pastry cut-out section of each shell. Carefully remove it or press it down into the shell. Spoon the hot chicken mixture into each pastry shell. Serve immediately.

Make ahead: This recipe is best made just before serving.
Serving suggestion: Serve with a green leaf salad drizzled with white wine vinaigrette.

Serves 6

cheese and spinach chicken roulade

mango chicken pastries

roasted pear and chicken salad

Serve this salad as an appetizer or a light lunch. If you are serving it as a main meal you may want to double the amount of chicken. Apple can be substituted for pear in this recipe.

SALAD
3 medium firm ripe pears, peeled
2 teaspoons canola oil, plus 1 tablespoon, extra
salt and cracked black pepper
1/2 cup granulated sugar
1/4 cup water
2/3 cup walnuts, toasted
pinch of ground cinnamon
1lb (500g) skinless, boneless chicken breasts
6 cups mixed baby lettuce leaves
4 oz (125g) creamy blue cheese, chopped

VINAIGRETTE
2 tablespoons finely chopped shallot
1/3 cup olive oil
2 tablespoons white wine vinegar
1 tablespoon honey
salt and cracked black pepper

To make the vinaigrette, put all the ingredients in a jar and shake until well combined.

To make the salad, line a baking sheet with parchment paper. Preheat the oven to 400°F (200°C).

Cut the pears lengthways into quarters and remove the cores. Cut each quarter in half. Place the pears, in a single layer, on the prepared baking sheet. Drizzle with 2 teaspoons of oil and sprinkle with salt and pepper to taste. Bake in the preheated oven for about 20 minutes, turning once during cooking, or until tender.

While the pears are cooking, stir the sugar and water in a small saucepan over medium-low heat until the sugar is dissolved. Turn the heat to high and boil, without stirring, for about 5 minutes or until golden, taking care not to let it burn. Place the walnuts close together on a greased baking sheet. Drizzle the walnuts with the sugar mixture and sprinkle with cinnamon. Let stand for about 15 minutes or until cool and hard; coarsely chop.

Place the chicken between 2 layers of plastic wrap. Using a rolling pin or the smooth side of a meat mallet, pound until about 1/2 inch (1cm) thickness. Sprinkle with salt and pepper. Heat the extra oil in a large frying pan over medium-high heat. Cook the chicken for 3 to 5 minutes on each side or until browned and tender.

Slice the chicken and arrange on individual serving plates with the pears, walnut toffee, lettuce leaves and blue cheese. Drizzle with the vinaigrette and serve.

Make ahead: The vinaigrette can be made 3 days ahead and stored in a jar in the refrigerator. Remove from the refrigerator 30 minutes before serving. The walnut toffee can be made a day ahead and stored in an airtight container, do not store it in the refrigerator.
Serving suggestions: Serve with warm crusty bread.

Serves 6

roasted pear and chicken salad

broccoli and cheese chicken parcels

peppercorn paprika chicken

broccoli and cheese chicken parcels

4 skinless, boneless chicken breasts
1 tablespoon canola oil
1/3 cup finely chopped onion
2/3 cup finely chopped broccoli
1 tablespoon all-purpose flour, plus 3 tablespoons extra
1/2 cup chicken broth (your own, see page 61 or store bought)

pinch of nutmeg
salt and cracked black pepper
1/2 cup white cheddar cheese
2 eggs, lightly beaten
1 1/2 cup panko breadcrumbs
2 tablespoons canola oil

Grease a baking sheet. Preheat the oven to 375°F (190°C).

Remove the tenderloins from each chicken breast and reserve for another use. Cut a pocket about 4 inches (10cm) long on the thickest side of each chicken breast, almost through to other side.

Heat the oil in a large frying pan over medium-high heat. Add the onion and broccoli cook, stirring occasionally, for about 5 minutes or until the onion is softened.

Stir in 1 tablespoon of flour and cook for 1 minute. Stir in the broth, nutmeg, salt and pepper and cook, stirring occasionally, for about 3 minutes or until thickened. Remove from the heat and add the cheese; cool. Spoon the mixture into each chicken breast (or place in a piping bag with a large nozzle and pipe into each pocket). Secure each pocket with toothpicks.

Coat each chicken breast in the extra flour. Dip in the egg and press into the breadcrumbs.

Heat the oil in a large frying pan and cook for about 5 minutes on each side until lightly browned. Place on the prepared baking sheet and cook in the preheated oven for about 15 minutes or until cooked and golden.

Make ahead: The chicken breasts can be prepared a day ahead and stored covered in the refrigerator. Remove from the refrigerator for 30 to 60 minutes before cooking.
Serving suggestion: Serve with garlic mashed potatoes, steamed spinach and lemon wedges.

Serves 4

peppercorn paprika chicken

You will find green peppercorns in a can in most grocery stores and specialty food stores.

4 split chicken breasts
1 teaspoon paprika
salt and cracked black pepper
1 tablespoon canola oil
2 garlic cloves, minced
1/3 cup brandy

3 tablespoons green peppercorns in brine, drained
1 cup chicken broth (your own, see page 61 or store bought)
1/2 cup whipping cream
2 tablespoons sour cream
1 teaspoon dijon mustard

Grease a baking sheet. Preheat the oven to 350°F (180°C).

Rub each piece of chicken with paprika and sprinkle with salt and pepper. Heat the oil in a large frying pan over medium heat. Add the chicken, bone side up, and cook for about 5 minutes on each side or until browned. Place on the prepared baking sheet and cook in the preheated oven for about 30 minutes or until tender.

Add the garlic to the same frying pan and cook over medium heat for about 2 minutes or until softened and fragrant.

Add the brandy and simmer for 5 minutes or until reduced by half (or carefully ignite the brandy and let the flames subside).

Add the remaining ingredients and cook, stirring occasionally, for 5 to 8 minutes or until the sauce is thickened. Drizzle the sauce over the chicken to serve.

Make ahead: This recipe is best made just before serving.
Serving suggestion: Serve with roasted rosemary, little new potatoes and sautéed spinach.

Serves 4

apricot glazed cornish hens with hazelnut stuffing

apricot glazed
cornish hens with hazelnut stuffing

HAZELNUT STUFFING
1 tablespoon butter
1/2 cup chopped onion
3 tablespoons apricot jam, warmed
2 cups coarse fresh breadcrumbs
3 tablespoons chopped fresh parsley
1/3 cup dried apricots, chopped
1/3 cup hazelnuts (filberts), toasted and chopped
1 tablespoon brandy (optional)
salt and cracked black pepper

APRICOT GLAZED CORNISH HENS
4 small Cornish hens
2 tablespoons butter
2 tablespoons apricot jam
1 tablespoon water
salt and cracked black pepper

To make the apricot hazelnut stuffing, heat the butter in a small frying pan over medium heat. Add the onion and cook, stirring occasionally, for about 5 minutes or until softened. Put into a medium bowl.

Add the remaining ingredients and stir to combine.

To make the apricot glazed Cornish hens, grease a wire rack and place inside a roasting pan lined with parchment paper. Preheat the oven to 350°F (180°C).

Rinse the hens inside and out with cold water and pat dry with paper towel. Fill the cavity of the hens with the stuffing and secure the opening with toothpicks. Tie the legs together and tuck the wings behind. Place the hens on the prepared rack. Roast the hens, uncovered, in the preheated oven for 50 minutes.

Melt the butter, jam and water in a small saucepan over low heat until melted. Brush the mixture over the hens and roast a further 10 minutes or until cooked and the juices run clear the when the chicken is pierced around the thigh bone (or when a meat thermometer reads 180°F (82°C), when inserted into the thickest part of the thigh).

Make ahead: The stuffing can be made up to 3 days ahead and stored in an airtight container in the refrigerator. Let stand at room temperature for 1 hour before stuffing the hens.
Serving suggestion: Serve with steamed Brussels sprouts drizzled with maple syrup and mashed orange sweet potato with a pinch of cinnamon.

Serves 4

quick and easy bake coating

This is enough to coat 1 1/2 lbs (750g) of chicken.

1 cup panko bread crumbs
2 tablespoons fine cornmeal (polenta)
1 teaspoon chicken bouillon powder

1/2 teaspoon celery salt
1/2 teaspoon cracked black pepper
1/2 teaspoon garlic powder

Put all the ingredients in a food processor. Process until well combined. Pour into a large re-sealable plastic bag. Add chicken pieces of your choice and toss to coat. Place the chicken on a greased rack on a baking sheet. Roast in 400°F (200°C) oven for 45 to 50 minutes until cooked and golden.

Make ahead: This coating can be made a month ahead and stored in an airtight container in a cool, dry place.
Makes about 2/3 cup

spiced crumb coating

This is enough to coat 4 chicken breasts.

1/2 teaspoon ground cumin
1/2 teaspoon ground coriander
1/4 teaspoon salt
1/4 teaspoon cracked black pepper
1/8 teaspoon ground cinnamon

1/8 teaspoon ground nutmeg
1/8 teaspoon ground cardamom
1 cup fine dry (or panko) breadcrumbs
2/3 cup pecans, toasted

Put all the ingredients in a food processor. Process until the nuts are finely chopped. Crumb the chicken and pan-fry or roast for about 15 minutes until golden.

Make ahead: This coating can be made a month ahead and stored in an airtight container in the freezer.
Makes about 1 1/2 cups

chili rub

This is enough to coat about 1 1/2 lbs (750g) chicken pieces or a whole chicken.

1 1/2 tablespoons chili powder
1 tablespoon garlic powder
1 tablespoon dried oregano
1 tablespoon paprika

1 teaspoon salt
1 teaspoon cracked black pepper
1 1/2 teaspoons granulated sugar

Combine all the ingredients in a small bowl. Rub over chicken pieces of your choice. Cover and marinate in the refrigerator for 3 hours or overnight. Pan-fry, broil, barbecue or roast the chicken until tender.

Make ahead: Store in a jar in a cool, dry place for up to 2 months.
Makes about 1/3 cup

cranberry wine sauce

Serve with roasted, grilled or pan-fried chicken. The sauce makes enough to serve 4 to 6 people.

1/3 cup cranberry jelly
1/2 cup dry white wine
2/3 cup chicken broth (your own,
   see page 61 or store bought)
1 rosemary sprig

1/4 teaspoon salt
1/4 teaspoon cracked black pepper
1 teaspoon cornstarch
1 tablespoon water
1 tablespoon butter

Combine jelly, wine, broth, rosemary, salt and pepper in a medium saucepan. Stir over medium heat until the jelly has melted. Let simmer, uncovered, for 10 minutes.

Combine the cornstarch and water in a small bowl. Stir into the cranberry jelly mixture. Stir until thickened slightly.

Whisk in butter and stir until melted.

Make ahead: This sauce is best made just before serving.
Makes about 1 cup

basil chili marinade
This is enough to marinate 1 lb (500g) of chicken.

1/3 cup dry white wine
3 tablespoons chopped fresh basil
1 tablespoon grainy mustard

2 tablespoons olive oil
1 teaspoon sambal oelek (chili paste)
2 garlic cloves, minced

Combine all the ingredients in a large, non-reactive bowl or re-sealable plastic bag. Add your favourite cut of chicken to the marinade. Stir or toss to combine. Cover or seal. Marinate the chicken for about 8 hours or overnight. Remove the chicken from the marinade and discard any marinade. Pan fry, broil or barbecue the chicken until tender.

Make ahead: This marinade can be made 2 days ahead and stored in an airtight container in the refrigerator.
Makes about 1/2 cup.

mushroom mustard sauce
Serve over roasted, grilled or pan-fried chicken. This makes enough sauce for 6 to 8 people.

1 tablespoon butter
2 teaspoons canola oil
2 cups sliced mushrooms
2 garlic cloves, minced
2 tablespoons all-purpose flour

1 cup chicken broth (your own, see page 61 or store bought)
2 tablespoons sour cream
2 teaspoons dijon mustard
salt and cracked black pepper, to taste

Heat the butter and oil in a large frying pan over medium-high heat. Add the mushrooms and garlic and cook, stirring occasionally, for about 5 minutes or until the mushrooms are softened.

Stir in the flour and cook, stirring, for 1 minute to cook the flour.

Add the remaining ingredients and boil gently, uncovered, stirring occasionally, for about 5 minutes or until thickened.

Make ahead: This sauce is best made just before serving.
Makes about 2 cups

marmalade and mustard glaze
This makes enough glaze for about 1 1/4 lbs (625g) chicken.

1/3 cup orange marmalade
2 tablespoons grainy mustard
1 tablespoons Worcestershire sauce

1 tablespoon onion powder
1 garlic clove, minced
1/4 teaspoon cracked black pepper

Combine all the ingredients in a small saucepan. Stir over medium-low heat for about 3 minutes or until melted. Brush over the chicken during the last 15 minutes of cooking.

Make ahead: This is best made just before using.
Makes about 1/2 cup

lemon grass and lime marinade
This is enough to marinate 1 lb (500g) of chicken pieces.

1/4 cup lime juice
1/4 cup chopped fresh cilantro
3 tablespoons Thai sweet chili sauce
2 tablespoons canola (or peanut) oil
2 tablespoons finely chopped lemon grass

1 tablespoon finely chopped ginger
2 teaspoons finely grated lime zest
1 teaspoon sesame oil
2 garlic cloves, minced
2 teaspoon fish sauce

Combine all the ingredients in a large, non reactive bowl or re-sealable plastic bag. Add the chicken pieces of your choice. Stir or toss to combine. Cover or seal. Marinate in the refrigerator for 8 hours or overnight. Remove chicken from the marinade and discard any marinade. Cook chicken on a barbecue, grill pan or roast in the oven until tender.

Make ahead: The marinade can be made 2 days ahead and stored in an airtight container in the refrigerator.
Makes about 1/2 cup

balsamic and rosemary marinade

This is enough to marinate 1lb (500g) of chicken pieces.

1/4 cup olive oil
1/4 cup balsamic vinegar
2 rosemary sprigs

1 tablespoon brown sugar
1/2 teaspoon cracked black pepper
6 garlic cloves, coarsely chopped

Combine all the ingredients in a large, non-reactive bowl or re-sealable plastic bag. Add the chicken pieces of your choice. Stir or toss to combine. Cover or seal. Marinate in the refrigerator for 8 hours or overnight. Remove chicken from the marinade and discard any marinade. Cook chicken on a barbecue, grill pan or roast in the oven until tender.

Make ahead: The marinade can be made 2 days ahead and stored in an airtight container in the refrigerator.
Makes about 1/2 cup

ginger and soy marinade

This is enough to marinate 1 lb (500g) chicken pieces.

1 tablespoon finely grated ginger
2 garlic cloves, minced
1 tablespoon canola oil
1/2 teaspoon Chinese five spice powder

1/4 cup soy sauce
1 tablespoon rice (or white wine) vinegar
1/4 cup finely chopped shallot
1 tablespoon honey

Combine all the ingredients in a large, non reactive bowl or re-sealable plastic bag. Add the chicken pieces of your choice. Stir or toss to combine. Cover or seal. Marinate in the refrigerator for 8 hours or overnight. Remove chicken from the marinade and discard any marinade. Cook chicken on a barbecue, grill pan or roast in the oven until tender.

Make ahead: The marinade can be made 2 days ahead and stored in an airtight container in the refrigerator.
Makes about 3/4 cup marinade

warm spice rub

This is enough to coat 1 1/2 lbs (750g) chicken pieces or 1 whole chicken.

1 small onion, chopped
2 tablespoons lemon juice
4 garlic cloves, minced
1 tablespoon white vinegar
1 tablespoon olive oil
1 tablespoon salt

1/2 teaspoon cracked black pepper
1/2 teaspooon cayenne pepper
1/2 teaspoon cinnamon
1/4 teaspoon nutmeg
1/4 teaspoon ground clove

Combine all the ingredients in a small bowl. Rub all over the chicken. Cover and marinate in the refrigerator for 3 hours or overnight. Pan-fry, broil, barbeque or roast the chicken until tender.

Make ahead: This rub can be made 2 weeks ahead and stored in an airtight container in the refrigerator.
Makes about 2/3 cup

citrus spice rub

This is enough to coat 1 1/2 lbs (750g) chicken pieces or a whole chicken.

1 tablespoon packed brown sugar
1 tablespoon finely grated orange zest
1 teaspoon finely grated lemon zest
1 teaspoon salt

1 teaspoon ground coriander
1 teaspoon garlic powder
1 teaspoon ground cumin
1/2 teaspoon cracked black pepper

Combine all the ingredients in a small bowl. Rub all over the chicken. Cover and marinate in the refrigerator for 3 hours or overnight. Pan-fry, broil, barbeque or roast the chicken until tender.

Make ahead: This rub can be made 2 weeks ahead and stored in an airtight container in the refrigerator.
Makes about 1/3 cup

rich tomato sauce

Serve over combined pasta and chicken, grilled or pan-fried chicken. This makes enough to serve 8 to 12 people.

10 medium ripe Roma tomatoes, halved lengthways
1/2 teaspoon salt
1/4 teaspoon cracked black pepper
1 tablespoon olive oil
1 cup chopped onion

2 garlic cloves, minced
2 tablespoons tomato paste
1 teaspoon balsamic vinegar
1 teaspoon packed brown sugar

Grease a wire rack and place on a baking sheet lined with parchment paper. Preheat the oven to 350°F (180°C).

Place the tomatoes, cut side up, on the prepared rack. Sprinkle with salt and pepper. Bake in the preheated oven for about 2 hours or until wilted and lightly browned. Put into a food processor.

Heat the oil in a large frying pan. Add the onion and garlic and cook, stirring occasionally, for about 5 minutes or until the onion is softened. Add to the tomatoes.

Add the remaining ingredients and process until almost smooth.

Make ahead: This sauce can be made 3 days ahead and stored in an airtight container in the refrigerator. Or, freeze for up to 3 months.
Makes about 3 cups

creamy dill and horseradish sauce

Serve with roasted, grilled or pan-fried chicken. This makes enough sauce for 4 to 6 people.

2 tablespoons butter
2 tablespoons finely chopped shallot
1 tablespoon all-purpose flour
2 tablespoons dry sherry

1 cup whipping cream
2 tablespoons creamed horseradish
2 tablespoons chopped fresh dill
salt and cracked black pepper

Melt the butter in a medium saucepan over medium heat. Add the shallot and cook for about 3 minutes or until softened.

Stir in the flour and cook, stirring, for 1 minute to cook the flour.

Add the sherry and stir until thickened. Add the remaining ingredients and stir until combined. Simmer, uncovered, for about 5 minutes or until thickened slightly.

Make ahead: This sauce is best made just before serving.
Makes about 1 cup

pesto, wine and garlic marinade

This is enough to marinate 1 lb (500g) of chicken.

1/3 cup basil pesto
1/3 cup dry white wine
1 tablespoon olive oil
1 tablespoon balsamic vinegar

6 garlic cloves, minced
1/2 teaspoon salt
1/2 teaspoon cracked black pepper

Combine all the ingredients in a large, non-reactive bowl or re-sealable plastic bag. Add your favourite cut of chicken to the marinade. Stir or toss to combine. Cover or seal. Marinate the chicken for about 8 hours or overnight. Remove chicken from the marinade and discard any marinade. Cook the chicken on a barbecue, grill pan or roast in the oven until tender.

Make ahead: This marinade can be made 2 days ahead and stored in an airtight container in the refrigerator.
Makes about 3/4 cup

index

index

chicken trivia

- Most of Alberta's 265 chicken farms are family owned and operated.

- In 2004, 117 million kgs of live weight of chicken was produced with a farm gate value of $143 million.

- Chickens raised for meat are not the same type of chickens that produce table eggs.

- Most of Alberta's chicken farmers produce 6 flocks of chicken a year.

- Most chicken, on average, will eat 4 kgs of feed in order to reach market size. For an average flock of 20,000 birds, over 80,000 or 6 1/2 truck loads of chicken feed is used!

- Per capita consumption of chicken in 2004 was 30.4 kgs.

- Chickens are housed in clean, well ventilated, climate-controlled barns where they are free to wander, drink and eat at will. The floor is generally covered with a litter of straw, paper or soft, dry wood shavings.

- Barns are thoroughly cleaned and disinfected after each flock is removed.

- Grain is the main ingredient of all chicken feed. All chickens in Canada are grain-fed.

- Chickens do not receive any hormones. The use of hormones in poultry is not allowed in Canada.

- A broiler usually weighs between 1.7 and 2.5 kg live weight and takes from 39 to 42 days to reach this weight.

nutritional information

- 100g serving of cooked chicken breast contains 2.1g fat; 33g protein; 159 calories.

- 100g serving of cooked chicken leg and thigh contains 6.9g fat; 25g protein; 170 calories.

- 100g lean ground chicken contains 12.4g fat; 22g protein; 207 calories.

- Canada's Food Guide recommends eating 2 to 3 servings of lean protein daily.